Lektürehilfen

Don DeLillo

Falling Man

von Elisabeth Kaltenbach

Klett Lerntraining

Elisabeth Kaltenbach, Gymnasiallehrerin für Deutsch und Englisch, Studiendirektorin am Weiterbildungskolleg (Abendgymnasium) Düsseldorf.

Die Seitenangaben zum Roman beziehen sich auf die Ausgaben:
Don DeLillo, *Falling Man,* New York: Scribner (export edition), 2008.
sowie auf:
Klettbuch 978-3-12-578859-6

Foto S. 11: The Associated Press GmbH (Richard Drew) Frankfurt am Main
S. 90: Giorgio Morandi: Still Life 1954 ©VG Bild-Kunst, Bonn 2009

9 783129 230534

Bibliografische Information der Deutschen Bibliothek
Die Deutsche Bibliothek verzeichnet diese Publikation in der Deutschen Nationalbibliografie; detaillierte bibliografische Daten sind im Internet über http://dnb.ddb.de abrufbar

Auflage 5. 4. 3. 2. 1. | 2013 2012 2011 2010 2009
Die letzten Zahlen bezeichnen jeweils die Auflage und das Jahr des Druckes.

Umschlagfoto: Interfoto München
Satz: DOPPELPUNKT, Stuttgart
Druck: Druck Partner Rübelmann, Hemsbach
Printed in Germany
ISBN 978-3-12-923053-4

Contents

I The Author and his Times

1. The Author's Life and Works

Don DeLillo was born on November 20, 1936 in the Bronx in New York City, into a working-class, Italian-American neighbourhood. He is a child of Italian immigrants; as a boy, his father came to the United States with his family from Abruzzi, Italy, in 1916. DeLillo's mother worked as a seamstress, his father, whom he describes as "a blue collar man who ended up wearing a suit", eventually became an auditor for Metropolitan Life Insurance Company. The DeLillo family lived in a small house, eleven of them, their speaking changed frequently from Italian to English and back, and his grandmother, who lived in America for fifty years, never really learned how to speak English.

As a child, DeLillo was not particularly interested in books, he led a street life and played all kinds of sports. (Sports figures prominently in some of his novels.) In 1954 he graduated from Cardinal Hayes High School in the Bronx ("I slept for four years there," Interview with Vince Passaro, 1991); only when he got a summer job as a parking attendant, he started to develop an interest in literature and spent many waiting hours reading novels by Henry James, William Faulkner, Ernest Hemingway. DeLillo says that he was not thinking of becoming a writer then, but that he "was beginning to sense the power of serious literature." (Interview with Mark Binelli, 2007) After his graduation from High School, DeLillo went to Fordham University, New York, where, he says, "I didn't study much of anything. I majored in something called communication arts" (Passaro, 1991); he earned his BA in 1958.

As he could not get one in publishing, he took up a job with Ogilvy & Mather, an advertising company, as a copywriter, writing image ads. In 1964, he left Ogilvy & Mather to become a freelance writer. When discussing the beginnings of his writing career, DeLillo mentions that he did some short stories at that time, but very infrequently: "I quit my job just to quit. I didn't quit my job to write fiction. I just didn't want to work anymore." (Passaro, 1991) Around 1966 he began working on his first novel, which took a long time as DeLillo had to take up all kinds of different jobs (e.g. writing about furniture or computers) to make a living. Finally, *Americana* was published in 1971, with rather moderate resonance. The novel follows the episodic adventures of a young television executive who leaves his job in order to travel the United States in search of himself. It is an early exploration of America and its national identity, a topic that has become one of the cornerstones of DeLillo's fiction. He says:

> "It's no accident that my first novel was called Americana. This was a private declaration of independence, a statement of my intention to use the whole picture, the whole culture. America was and is the immigrant's dream, and as the son of two immigrants I was attracted by the sense of possibility that had drawn my grandparents and parents." (Interview with Adam Begley, 1993)

The first book was followed by *End Zone* (1972), a novel that features a college football team and a meditation on nuclear war, and *Great Jones Street* (1973), about rock music and drugs.

In 1975, DeLillo married Barbara Bennett, a former banker, now a landscape designer; the couple lived in Toronto, Canada, for a year when she worked for Citibank there. He started reading about mathematics, as he wanted to gain a fresh view of the world, to immerse himself in something as remote as possible from his own interests and work. Becoming really fascinated by the beauty of scientific language, the mystery of numbers, he ended up writing a novel about mathematicians, *Ratner's Star*, which was published in 1976. His fifth novel, *Players* (1977), for the first time takes up the subject of terrorism: It is about a young urban couple in New York; the man is getting involved with a terrorist group plotting to blow up the New York Stock Exchange, where he works; the woman works for a firm called the Grief Management Council, based in the World Trade Center – in retrospect, some uncanny foreshadowings of future events. The book's successor, *Running Dog*, published in 1978, also provides elements of spying and thriller fiction, as it describes the search by reporters and intelligence agents for a pornographic film that Hitler allegedly made in the last days of World War II.

In 1979, DeLillo won a Guggenheim Fellowship that allowed him to go abroad for about three years; he spent the time living in Greece and travelling through the Middle East and India, also working on his next novel, *The Names*, which was then published in 1982. Back in the USA, he reflected on the importance of those years for his biography and writing:

> "What I found was that all this traveling taught me how to see and hear all over again. Whatever idea about language may be in *The Names*, I think the most important thing is what I felt in hearing people and watching them gesture – in listening to the sound of Greek and Arabic and Hindu and Urdu. The simple fact that I was confronting new landscapes and fresh languages made me feel almost duty bound to get it right. I would see and hear more clearly than I could in more familiar places." (Interview with Robert Harris, 1982)

So far DeLillo had been praised by critics, but had not really reached a widespread readership; this changed dramatically with the publication of his eighth novel, *White Noise*, in 1985. This book about a university professor and his consumer-oriented family in a middle-American town features a chemical spill, an "airborne toxic event", as the media call it, caused by an industrial accident. The novel combines some of DeLillo's most prominent themes: the fear of death, the culture of celebrity, the influence of the mass media, especially the central position of television, which almost becomes a character in the family. *White Noise* won the National Book Award in 1986. Similar praise was given to DeLillo's next two novels, *Libra* (1988), a fictional portrait of Lee Harvey Oswald, who shot President John F. Kennedy in 1963, and *Mao II* (1991), a story about a reclusive novelist who becomes involved in events surrounding a terrorist group and a poet held hostage in Beirut.

In 1997, DeLillo published *Underworld*, his longest, most complicated and most highly praised novel, considered his 'magnum opus' so far. Covering nearly half a century from 1951 till 1992, the book presents a panorama of American characters and landscapes and portrays the country's vastness and the varieties of American life and culture from the mid to the late 20th century; it is also a reflection on the history of the Cold War. The novel was DeLillo's biggest mainstream success, it was awarded the Jerusalem Prize at the Jerusalem International Book Fair in 1999, the Howells Medal by the American Academy of Arts and Letters in 2000 and marked, as critic and writer Martin Amis put it, "the ascension of a great writer". (To add to DeLillo's allegedly prophetic imagination and writing, the original cover of the novel shows the twin towers of the World Trade Center in the mist, in the foreground a bird with spreaded wings flying towards them.)

DeLillo's masterpiece of some 800 pages was followed by two novels that are considered of lesser range and quality: *The Body Artist* (2001), a dark and brief quasi-ghost story, and *Cosmopolis* (2003), about a young Manhattan billionaire and an economic collapse caused by the breakdown of the Japanese Yen. In this book the author wanted to capture the atmosphere and enormous economic optimism of March and April 2000 and counter it with a fatal crash of the stock market (again, an uncanny vision of the future).

DeLillo was in the middle of writing *Cosmopolis*, when the terror attacks on the USA on September 11, 2001 occurred. Having lived in New York City for nearly all his life, he was extremely stunned by the traumatic events and stopped working for a while. Together with his editor, who lived downtown Manhattan and was allowed to pass the barricades, he visited Ground Zero a few days later with the vague intention of writing an essay about the attacks.

(This long essay with the title "In the Ruins of the Future" was eventually published in *Harper's Magazine* in December 2001.) Yet he was not finished with the events: He was thinking as a novelist, not (only) as an essayist: "I needed to see things, to literally smell things. I wanted to start at street level." (Binelli, 2007) An image formed in his mind: a man covered with dust and ash, walking in the streets of Manhattan – the introductory scene of *Falling Man*. It took DeLillo more than three years, till November 2004, the day after George W. Bush's re-election (as the writer clearly remembers), to start working on his latest novel, which was eventually published in June 2007.

Don DeLillo, who also wrote stories, four plays and a screenplay, *Game 6* (written in the early 1990s, made into a film by director Michael Hoffman, starring Michael Keaton, in 2005), has always emphasized the importance of New York City for his life and writing: "I became a writer by living in New York and seeing and hearing and feeling all the great, amazing and dangerous things the city endlessly assembles." (Interview with Jonathan Bing, 1997)

DeLillo is generally named as one of the great American novelists of his time, together with Thomas Pynchon, Philip Roth, Cormac McCarthy. He has influenced many of the younger English-language authors, such as Jonathan Franzen and the late David Foster Wallace. He is friends with many authors, for example Paul Auster, to whom he dedicated his novel *Cosmopolis*, but he is eager to tell that this does not mean that they talk about their work all the time: "We rather talk about other, quite ordinary things. I talk a lot about movies and sports with Paul. We both like baseball. I'm actually quite happy to occupy myself with something else." (Interview with Peter Henning, 2003)

2. The Background of the Novel

2.1 The Terror Attacks on September 11, 2001

No other historic event since the Japanese surprise bombing of the US military base in Pearl Harbor in December 1941, during World War II, has had such a deep and devastating impact on the American nation (and indeed on the whole world) like the terror attacks on September 11, 2001. Almost simultaneously, a group of nineteen Arabic terrorists, headed by Mohamed Atta, hijacked four American airliners and re-directed them to New York and Washington. The terrorists, many of whom had been living and studying in

Hamburg in the 1990s, had done a special flight training in the USA, mainly in Florida. They belonged to the Islamist group al-Quaeda, whose head and leading strategist, Osama bin Laden, almost certainly pulled the strings behind the 9/11 attacks.

Chronology of the Events

At 8:45 a.m. American Airlines Flight 11, a Boeing 767 hijacked en route from Boston to Los Angeles with 92 passengers and crew aboard, and most probably piloted by Mohamed Atta, slammed into the north tower of the World Trade Center in New York. At first safety authorities believed in a fatal accident. At 9:06 a.m., however, United Airlines Flight 175, also a Boeing 767 hijacked en route from Boston to Los Angeles with 65 passengers and crew aboard, sliced through the south tower – and made everybody realize this was a terrorist attack. Shortly after that, at 9:40 a.m. American Airlines Flight 77, a Boeing 757 hijacked en route from Washington, D.C., to Los Angeles with 64 people aboard, was redirected to Washington and crashed into the Pentagon, the U.S. Ministery of Defense. All U.S. airports were shut down, planes already in the air were forced to return to the nearest airport to land. At 10:00 a.m. the south tower of the World Trade Center collapsed; weakened by the imploding of its twin, the north tower collapsed at 10:29 a.m.. At 10:37 a.m. United Airlines Flight 93, another Boeing 757 hijacked en route from Newark International Airport to San Francisco with 45 people aboard, crashed in Shanksville, Pennsylvania, eighty miles southeast of Pittsburgh. It is believed that its target was Washington, too, probably the White House or the Capitol, but some passengers, who knew about the attack on the World Trade Center from phone calls to their families and realized that they were going to die anyway, started to fight the hijackers, which finally caused the plane to crash in a field, only a few miles away from the next town. Finally, at 5:25 p.m. a third building in the World Trade Center complex in New York City collapsed.

More than 3,000 people lost their lives in the attacks, most of them in the twin towers. September 11, 2001 ist generally seen as a turning-point in history, the beginning of an "age of terrorism" on a scale not known before. It has determined U.S. politics ever since: October 2001 brought the American invasion in Afghanistan ("Enduring Freedom") to catch Bin Laden, remove al-Quaeda forces and oust the Taliban regime. Although the latter aim was achieved, Bin Laden has never been found and Afghanistan remains a place of unstableness and insecurity. In March 2003, American troops, mainly supported by the British, went into Iraq; Saddam Hussein was seen as a threat, as he was supposed to have weapons of mass destruction that he could use to aid terrorist groups. Although Saddam's regime was quickly toppled, he himself was later caught and sentenced to death by the new Iraqi government, the situation in the country has been more than tense with violent insurgencies. The attitude of the American public has long changed: Now most of the Americans strongly oppose the war in Iraq and demand a withdrawal of their troops.

2.2 Richard Drew's Photo of the Falling Man

September 11, 2001 is certainly the most media-processed day in the world's history, pictures being printed and televised endlessly and repeatedly. There is one photo, however, that has become one of the most outstanding and most disputed: the picture known as "The Falling Man", taken at 9:41 a.m. by the American professional photographer Richard Drew. It shows a man who is falling head-first from the north tower of the World Trade Center, one knee bent, his body almost like an arrow in front of the vertical lines of the twin towers behind him. Most probably he is one of the more than two hundred people (called "jumpers" by the press) who were trapped on the upper floors of the towers and apparently chose to jump rather than die from the fire and smoke.

Richard Drew, who had been working for Associated Press for more than thirty years, had photographed historic moments in American history before; he was, for example, one of the few photographers who took pictures the moment Robert Kennedy was shot in Los Angeles in 1968. On the morning of September 11 he was taking photos on a maternity fashion show when news came out that a plane had crashed into the World Trade Center. Immediately Drew hurried downtown, and when he arrived at the scenery, both towers already were on fire. He started taking pictures of the debris and people who were in shock, then he had to change places to where the ambulances were. A policeman suddenly pointed to the building and they saw several people falling off the north tower. Drew never stopped photographing, his camera always taking photos in a row when he held his finger on the trigger. Only after both towers had collapsed, he had to run away with all the other people. Back in the office of Associated Press, he looked at the sequences he had shot and immediately knew which one to choose for publication: the picture of the falling man. The next morning it appeared in the *New York Times* and many other newspapers all over the country and caused highly critical and furious reactions among readers, who complained that it violated the dying man's privacy or exploited a man's death. Thus in most American newspapers the photo ran only once and never again. "In the most photographed and videotaped day in the history of the world, the images of people jumping were the only images that became, by consensus, taboo – the only images from which Americans were proud to avert their eyes." (Tom Junod, "The Falling Man", in: *Esquire*, September 2003)

Richard Drew maintains that people's strong reactions show how important his picture is and he thinks that it has nothing to do with voyeurism or exploitation: " 'I didn't capture this person's death. I captured part of his life. This is what he decided to do, and I think I preserved that.' " (Peter Howe, "Richard Drew", in: *The Digital Journalist*, December 2001)
The identity of the man in the photo has never been clarified with absolute certainty, but – despite all the criticism – the photo has become an icon and gained a symbolic quality for man's destiny in general, the falling through time and space towards an end.

II The Plot

Falling Man deals with one of the most tragic and defining events in recent American history, the terror attacks on September 11, 2001, yet it does not turn out to be the novel that some of the readers might have expected from its author. Instead of mingling historical characters with fictional story lines in a broad, panoramic way (as, for example, in his books *Libra* and *Underworld*), DeLillo here chooses a different way of addressing that fatal day and its aftermath. He focuses on a couple, their child and some people around them from the moment the twin towers of the World Trade Center collapse to the Iraq War protests in New York City in 2004. Thus the novel consists of three parts, covering the periods of a few days, a few weeks and some three years after the attacks.

Thirty-nine-year-old Keith Neudecker escapes from the north tower, where he has been working as a lawyer for a decade, shortly before it comes down on September 11. Covered in ash and blood, with only a minor wrist injury, he impulsively turns up at the flat of his wife Lianne, from whom he has been separated for some time, and his seven-year-old son Justin. Lianne takes him in, slowly they start to share a marriage again.

On his way down the staircase in the north tower, Keith has grasped a stranger's briefcase. It belongs to a woman called Florence Givens, who worked on a different floor. After finding out her address and that she, too, has survived, Keith goes to see her to return the briefcase. They talk, meet again, have a short affair – mainly because it gives them both the opportunity to speak about their experiences and to feel some kind of consolation.

Keith's wife Lianne, who works as a freelance editor, was not in the towers when they fell, but her life is equally out of balance. Haunted by memories of her father, who killed himself because of beginning dementia, and by her own fear of that disease, she leads a writing group for early-stage Alzheimer's patients in a community centre in East Harlem. Lianne seems almost obsessed with the terror attacks and their effects on her life, her city and the people around her. She takes in all the news stories about the victims and encourages the members of the group to write not only about their lives, but also about their experiences of that special day. A neighbour playing loud Arabic-sounding music makes Lianne increasingly aggressive so that one day she even attacks the woman physically.

At the same time both Keith and Lianne have to deal with the fears of their son Justin, who – staring through binoculars with two friends from the 27th floor of their high rise flat – keeps scanning the sky for more planes sent by an unknown enemy.
Lianne frequently visits her mother Nina, a former university professor of art, who is increasingly suffering from the burden of old age. In the wake of the terror attacks, Nina engages in fervent political discussions with her lover Martin, a somewhat shady European art dealer, who later turns out to have been at least loosely connected with a German terrorist group in the 1970s.
Twice in the weeks after September 11, Lianne encounters a performance artist known as Falling Man, who turns up unexpectedly in several parts of the city, jumps headfirst from high places in a business suit, held only by a safety harness – thus enacting the famous photo of a man jumping from one of the burning towers shortly after it was hit by the plane and generally bringing back memories of all the other people who did the same.
Three years have passed, when the last part of the novel begins. Lianne's mother Nina has died, Justin is developing into a somewhat difficult teenager. By chance, Lianne sees Falling Man's obituary in a newspaper: He died at the age of 39, of natural causes.
Keith and Lianne are now leading an on-and-off relationship: Keith has not returned to his job, but taken up a life as a professional poker player, partly in memory of the regular Wednesday night poker games with some male friends two of whom lost their lives in the towers on September 11. He spends his time in places like Las Vegas and Atlantic City, only sporadically coming home to his wife and son for a few days. Lianne, still worrying about her health and missing her mother and her Alzheimer's patients group, seeks comfort in regularly going to a church and generally tries to settle into a calm and reliable life with her son.

At the end of each of the three parts of the novel, Keith's and Lianne's story is left and the reader is taken into the mind of Hammad, a member of the Hamburg cell of the 9/11 terrorists, thus getting to know the young Arab's doubts, worldly wishes and urges and final resolve and readiness for the task ahead of him. The reader follows Hammad from his flat in Hamburg to Florida, where the terrorists do their flight training, to his last moments in the plane that crushes into the north tower of the World Trade Center. Here the narrator swings back to Keith Neudecker, rendering a detailed account of the apocalyptic situation in the tower after the attack and Keith's narrow escape. The end of the novel returns to the beginning, the circle is closed.

III The Story

As mentioned above, *Falling Man* consists of three parts, either using Keith's or Lianne's perspective to narrate their story (except the three appendices, which are Hammad's). Apart from the first two chapters, however, the narration neither follows a chronological order nor does it remain consistent with one perspective in each chapter. On the contrary, there is a continuous cross-cutting between Keith's and Lianne's perspective, there is also a frequent change between the present situation and flashbacks, memories of past events. The different scenes vary considerably in length; sometimes there are deliberately vague pronoun references so that the reader may find it difficult to establish who is speaking.
As a help, the following summaries do not follow the order presented in the chapters, but try to re-organize the contents according to the perspectives used. (For an overview of the real structure and a table of the alternating scenes of each chapter see Appendix, pp. 98–103.)

Part One: Bill Lawton

Chapter 1

The first sentence of the novel takes the reader right into the inferno: "It was not a street anymore but a world, a time and space of falling ash and near night." (p. 3) A man in a suit, carrying a briefcase, covered with dust, glass and blood, is walking away from the collapsing twin towers of the World Trade Center, his place of work. It is through the eyes of this man, 39-year-old lawyer Keith Neudecker on his walk north, that all the images, sounds, even smells of the terror attacks on the morning of September 11, 2001 are evoked again, in a very specific, personal, almost intimate way. "The roar was still in the air, the buckling rumble of the fall. This was the world now." (ibid.) This first chapter presents an overwhelming amount of impressions and observations, registered in the senses and filtered in the mind of one man. Keith takes in all the details, the smoke, the debris, all the office paper coming down, policemen and security guards running towards the towers and people drenched in water from the sprinkling systems, who have escaped from the towers just like him. He also sees people who jump or fall, "figures in windows a thousand feet up, dropping into free space" (p. 4), and in the middle of chaos, there is one observation that seems to have a strong impact on him, as can be seen in the detailed description:

> "There was something else then, outside all this, not belonging to this, aloft. He watched it coming down. A shirt came down out of the high smoke, a shirt lifted and drifting in the scant light and then falling again, down toward the river." (ibid.)

Keith finds himself among other people running away, fighting for breath, cursing and shouting in disbelief, and he sees passers-by, joggers and members of a tai chi group, who watch the scenery in utter shock and horror.
A woman with a dust mask hands Keith a bottle of water. He realizes that he does not use his left arm, which probably means that he is injured, but he drinks the water thankfully before going on, still carrying the briefcase.
The description of the chaotic scenery continues, Keith hears the sound of the "second fall", i.e. the collapse of the second tower. He begins to see his surroundings in an increasingly strange and unusual way; it seems as if the world has been turned upside down, the things have lost their usual meaning, importance, purpose:

> "There was something critically missing from the things around him. They were unfinished, whatever that means. They were unseen, whatever that means, shop windows, loading platforms, paint-sprayed walls. Maybe this is what things look like when there is no one here to see them." (p. 6)

Keith, on hearing the second tower fall, has problems to disconnect, to accept his real situation as being more or less safely outside the tower: "That was him coming down, the north tower" (ibid.); and later: "He tried to tell himself he was alive but the idea was too obscure to take hold." (p. 7) At the end of the chapter he is picked up by a truck driver who asks him where he wants to go and he finally realizes what his destination has been all along.

Chapter 2

The second chapter introduces Keith's estranged wife Lianne (as the reader realizes only gradually); it is related exclusively from her perspective. At the beginning her mind wanders to the early times of their marriage, eight years ago, when their relationship was exciting and charged with their mutual sexual attraction. Lianne is brought back to present reality by a postcard she has received from a friend on holiday in Rome. It is a reproduction of the cover of *Revolt of Islam*, a poem in twelve cantos by the English writer Percy Bysshe Shelley (1792–1822). Although Lianne realizes that the card was sent a week or two ago, she immediately connects it to the terror attacks, thus showing the overpowering influence on her everyday life and concept of time: "This was all, a lost moment on the Friday of that lifelong week, three days after the planes." (p. 10)

Lianne goes to see her mother Nina, a retired professor of art, who has recently undergone knee-replacement surgery and is now "finally and resolutely old" (p. 11). Nina's tastefully designed and decorated apartment near Fifth Avenue in Manhattan, usually tidy and almost like a museum, is now "in a state of happy disarray" (p. 10) because of toys and games scattered all over the floor. They belong to Lianne's son Justin, who turns out to have been at his grandmother's flat when his father Keith showed up at Lianne's and Justin's home right after his escape from the World Trade Center that week. The conversation between Lianne and Nina circles around Keith and Lianne's past and present feelings for him, but also her worries about the future. Nina wants to know why Keith has come to Lianne's of all places and if they have discussed their situation. Lianne, who knows about her mother's reserve towards Keith, ironically defends Keith's former "reticence" in the presence of his dominant mother-in-law, whereas Nina in return warns her daughter not to let the exceptional situation, "sympathy and goodwill" (p. 12) interfere with her former decision to separate from Keith.

Lianne thinks how much her mother's physical ailment has changed her and how she tries, if ironically, to cope with old age. Together the two women recall their feelings and those of all the other people watching the towers fall and fearing their loved ones are dead. As a kind of contrasting image, Lianne reflects on her mother's habit to walk to the Metropolitan Museum and look at pictures for hours, as if in search of something stable and unchanging. "She looked at what was unfailing. She liked the big rooms, the old masters, what was unfailing in its grip on the eye and mind, on memory and identity." (p. 13) Lianne herself especially likes two still lifes by the Italian painter Giorgio Morandi in her mother's flat, which she finds mysterious and moving.

Nina goes on criticizing Lianne's motivation to marry Keith in the first place, namely to "feel dangerously alive" (p. 14), and descibes him as a man only "built for weekends" (p. 15) Lianne retorts that her mother's sole objection to Keith is his not being a scholar or an artist. The argument is ended for the time being when the buzzer sounds and the doorman announces Nina's lover Martin.

Chapter 3

(From now on there is a continuous change of scenes taking up either Keith's or Lianne's story line and perspective; sometimes the lines connect.)

The beginning of the chapter returns to the immediate aftermath of the terror attacks by presenting **Keith** in hospital for a complete check-up of his actual and possible injuries, with other wounded people on gurneys and in wheelchairs around him. After a thorough examination a young doctor takes the splinters of glass out of his face and informs him that the worst cases are in downtown hospitals and that there are less survivors turning up than they expected. He also tells Keith a horrid story about "organic shrapnel", tiny body fragments of suicide bombers, literally ripped to pieces by the explosion, that are driven into the skin of people nearby.
Later Keith is lying within a closed unit for a scan and despite the reassuring remarks of the Russian radiologist in charge of the test he feels deeply uncomfortable in the tube. Neither the classical music he has chosen nor the thoughts of two women, both called Nancy, that he had affairs with some time ago, help him to overcome his uneasiness with the noise and the feeling of being trapped. Instead, the doctor's remarks remind him of dying and are immediately associated with his experiences in the towers: "But that was another matter, wasn't it, in another kind of noise, and the trapped man does not come sliding out of his tube." (p. 22)

Keith has to undergo some simple surgery on his injured wrist, and although he has received shots for sedation and memory suppression, he sees images of his friend Rumsey in the tower shortly after the attack, "Rumsey in the smoke, things coming down." (p. 26)
Presumably a few days later, Keith is on his way to his apartment where he used to live on his own after his separation from Lianne and Justin. As it is very close to Ground Zero (this expression never falls), the whole area is completely closed off by military police and troops. While Keith repeatedly tries to pass the checkpoints, presenting a heart-rending story of cats to feed and unhappy children, the reader gets a detailed and vivid impression of the setting after the attacks, of the heavy machinery and the people that have to work in the remains of the towers and to clean up the surroundings. There are only few civilians with dust masks that Keith meets once he has been allowed to enter the "frozen zone" (p. 29). When he finally sees the remains of the towers, Keith is hit by the full impact of the catastrophe:

> "He stood at the National Rent-A-Fence barrier and looked into the haze, seeing the strands of bent filigree that were the last standing things, a skeletal remnant of the tower where he'd worked for ten years. The dead were everywhere, in the air, in the rubble, on rooftops nearby, in the breezes that carried from the river. They were settled in ash and drizzled on windows all along the streets, in his hair and on his clothes." (p. 30)

He is joined by a man who talks about where he was and what he did when "it happened" and then speaks with somebody else on the phone, his feelings summed up in the sentence: " 'I'm standing here.' " (p. 31) After another warning by policemen, who tell him that the tower at One Liberty Plaza is about to fall down, Keith finally reaches his apartment building, which seems to be empty. He does not take the elevator, but walks up the stairs to his flat on the ninth floor. When he enters and realizes that nothing has changed apart from the dirt and grime on his windows, he seems to have a close look at his place for the first time in one and a half years. The only importance it holds for him is its having been the site of the weekly poker game with his friends, "the one uncomplicated interval of his week, his month, […] – the one anticipation that was not marked by the bloodguilt tracings of severed connections." (p. 33) With "two players dead, one badly injured" (ibid.) in the towers (as the reader must presume), Keith will not need the poker table any more; he only takes a suitcase with a few clothes and important documents before leaving his apartment for good. Again avoiding the elevator (he confesses to himself that he is scared of using it), he walks down the stairs and away from the building, all the time accompanied by the sounds and noise of the rescue work at Ground Zero. After he has collected his undelivered mail at the local post office, Keith shows some bitter kind of irony when he thinks that "it might be hard to find a taxi at a time when every cabdriver in New York was named Muhammad." (p. 34)

Lianne meets Isabel, the mother of Justin's best friends, a sister and a brother, whom they have started to call the Siblings; they live in a high-rise. Isabel is worried because she has been watching the three children standing at a window, being secretive about something, mentioning a man's name. She asks Lianne if she knows what they are on about, if Justin has told her anything, but Lianne does not have a clue. As a rather lame explanation she mentions Justin's interest in the weather; she genererally does not take the situation too seriously: "Lianne wasn't sure what this was all about. It was about three kids being kids together." (p. 20) –
A scene in Lianne's bedroom shows her getting dressed and Keith watching

her. Lianne reflects on Keith's appearance ("still in shape and beginning to look seasoned", ibid.) and on the present state of their relationship. They sleep in the same bed, he talks and mostly listens, Lianne feels comfortable with the situation. She knows that they will also have sex again some day. – Lianne studies the expression on the face of one of the nineteen terrorists, "the man from Flight 11" (p. 23) in the newspaper.
Later she receives a phone call from Carol Shoup, an executive editor in a large publishing house, whom Lianne works for from time to time. Carol, who sent the postcard from Rome with the cover of Shelley's poem *Revolt of Islam*, carefully asks if this is a bad time and should they talk later? This reminds Lianne of similarly tactful remarks of all the people calling after Keith's return to his family and of her own angry, reserved reactions to those calls. She thinks that Keith prefers not to go out and be with other people: "This is where he wanted to be, outside the tide of voices and faces, God and country, sitting alone in still rooms, with those nearby who mattered." (p. 24) During the phone call Lianne hears some music somewhere in the building, she goes to the door and listens.
In another scene in their bedroom Lianne finally asks Keith why he has come to her flat, if it was because of Justin; she confesses to herself that this explanation would not be enough for her, that she "needed to hear something beyond this, a broader motive for his action or intuition" (p. 25). Keith does not have a rational explanation, he only tells her how he was picked up by the van driver after he had escaped from the tower and that the driver had no idea what had happened as his radio had been stolen from the van. The driver only saw that one of the twin towers was missing and later, after he had picked up Keith, that the second tower was gone, too. Keith emphasizes that he did not want to be taken to hospital but expressly gave the driver Lianne's address to go there; this makes Lianne feel better.
On another day she steps into the street, all the time trying to get a grip on her present life and situation by following a daily routine: "dinner, dry cleaning, cash machine, that's it, go home." (p. 26) But her mind is wandering crisscross, she thinks of the work she has to do (editing a book on ancient alphabets, written by a Bulgarian in English), of the food she wants to give Justin; then she stops right in the middle of the avenue, with taxis speeding towards her, "to work out her fate" (p. 27). For some reason she remembers a sign for "ethnic shampoo" she read in a shop window in Santa Fé when she was travelling in New Mexico with a man she had a short affair with during the separation. When Lianne runs toward the other side of the street, she seems to feel incoherent, unstable, in need of protection: "how good it felt,

hiding behind the plastic shimmer of the dry cleaner's long sheath, which she held at arm's length, between her and the taxis, in self-defense." (pp. 27–28) She still does not know if and how to deal with the new situation and Keith's presence; neither is she able to rationally explain to herself why she has to think of "ethnic shampoo, in the middle of Third Avenue" (p. 28). This remains as indecipherable to her as the unreadable author's emendations in the manuscript she has to edit.

Chapter 4

As a regular commitment comparable to Keith's weekly poker game, **Lianne** has established a writing group with men and women in the early stages of Alzheimer's disease, taking place in a community centre in East Harlem. The meetings follow a strict schedule: After having talked about events in the world or their lives, Lianne hands out writing pads and pens, suggests a topic or makes them choose one themselves, they write for about twenty minutes and then read aloud what they have written. Although sometimes their writing already shows signs of their progressing disease, they share many happy moments: "They laughed loud and often. They worked into themselves, finding narratives that rolled and tumbled, and how natural it seemed to do this, tell stories about themselves." (p. 36) The members, named Rosellen, Benny, Omar, Carmen, Anna, Curtis, of course write about many different things – but shortly after the terror attacks all of them, even Omar, who feels nervous about it at first, insist on writing about "the planes".
Ten days after the attacks (within the story, time is always measured by "days after the planes") Lianne walks to Grand Central Station to meet her mother, who has been away for a few days with her lover Martin. Lianne notices that the number of police and state troopers has increased considerably. Suddenly her attention is caught by something outside the station, people crowding and traffic building up. When she steps outside, she sees a man in a business suit dangling headfirst on a safety harness from a steel structure high above the street. Standing among the watchers, some of them shouting at the man furiously, Lianne remembers that she has heard of him, a performance artist called Falling Man. After the terror attacks he has already appeared in several places around the city performing his act and thus bringing back the dreadful images of the people who fell or jumped from the burning towers. Lianne picks up her mother, who tells her that she did not want to stay away from New York and her apartment any longer, and leads her away from the main entrance in order to avoid the spectacle of the Falling Man.

Lianne again reflects on the state of her relationship with Keith. They still do not have sex, but this is not a problem for either of them. Lianne realizes that it takes time, that they live in an exceptional situation, the only clear feeling being: “She wanted contact and so did he.” (p. 43)

Once more Lianne meets the Siblings’ mother, this time in a bakery, where she is waiting to be served. Isabel again tries to question her about the secret doings of the three children. It seems that Justin always brings along binoculars (presumably Keith’s) to watch something outside, while they keep talking about a man called Bill Lawton. And again Lianne, who wants to get out of the situation quickly, states that Justin has not told her anything and she can only presume it has to do with their school work.
However, later she goes to Justin’s room to ask her son about the binoculars that he has taken without Keith’s permission and the man he and the Siblings keep talking about. Justin, who is sharpening pencils (he seems to collect special ones as a sort of status symbol), does not answer her questions but reacts as if he does not know what she is talking about.
In a flashback, the reader learns that Lianne’s father, Jack Glenn, killed himself with a shotgun sixteen years ago because he did not accept “the long course of senile dementia” (p. 50). Lianne, who then was twenty-two, has always wondered if he killed himself with the gun that he gave her once to hold when she visited him in New Hampshire where he was living, separated from his wife and daughter. It seems that Lianne enjoyed the times she could spend with her father; she liked going to the woods with him and his way of explaining technical structures, such as cars, motorcycles, guns. The words “muzzle blast” have remained in her memory – they are a constant reminder of his death and her wish to believe that it was brave to kill himself.
The following scene is probably a continuation of a scene in chapter 2, with Lianne being in her mother’s flat and greeting Martin Ridnour, her mother’s lover, who has just returned from Europe on one of the first transantlantic flights resumed after the terror attacks. They talk about the events and possible reactions to them. Martin, an art dealer, whose whereabouts and personal situation are unclear to Lianne, tells her that he is going away with Nina to a house in Connecticut for a few weeks. Lianne asks him if he still has sex with her mother; Martin evades the question and asks her about the situation with Keith in return. When Lianne’s mother comes in, she starts to quiz Martin about his dealings in Europe. Later she provokes a political discussion with her lover, whereas Lianne silently keeps aside with the familiar feeling of “how Nina at a certain point began to consider her invisible.”

(pp. 57–58) She knows that she has not lived up to her mother's expectations in the past:

> "Lianne's studies were meant to take her into deeper scholarship, into serious work in language or art history. She'd traveled through Europe and much of the Middle East but it was tourism in the end, with shallow friends, not determined inquiry into beliefs, institutions, languages, art, or so said Nina Bartos." (p. 58)

Nina argues that the terrorists do not follow any religious or political aim, but only kill innocent people out of sheer panic. In Martin's opinion, they consider Western societies to be sick and they want to show the vulnerability of a seemingly invincible power such as the USA. For him, the attacks are a consequence of a long period of suffering from injustice and poverty. Nina, who is getting more and more angry and agitated, denies Western responsibility for the events and claims that the societies the terrorists have come from have been pulled down by their own incapabilities to cope with life and their circumstances: "'It's their own history, their mentality. They live in a closed world, of choice, of necessity. They haven't advanced because they haven't wanted to or tried to.'" (p. 59) At some point Lianne leaves the room and spends some time in the bathroom, again trying to come to terms with her situation, with Keith back in her and her son's life. When she returns, the argument between her mother and Martin has subsided, Nina being on the brink of sleep and Martin looking intently at one of Morandi's still lifes on the wall. The painting shows a collection of kitchen objects, among them two tall, dark items that remind Martin of the twin towers. Lianne steps forward to have a look herself and agrees: "She saw what he saw. She saw the towers." (p. 62)

After having left his own apartment for good, **Keith** returns to their flat uptown and sorts through his mail. His last name, Neudecker, is misspelled on some of the letters, which he seems to be used to. He makes corrections on the envelopes and reflects on this habit, when and why he started doing it. Keith only knows that he will probably continue doing it in the future – which means that he actually thinks about a future at all. He does not make corrections on junk mail (this seems inadequate) and always hides the act of correcting. –

Keith sees a small briefcase on the closet floor and slowly realizes that it is neither his nor Lianne's; he vaguely remembers having taken it, "an object pale with ash", on his escape from the tower. After some hesitation, he opens it and examines its contents, many different things such as headphones and

CD player, pen, notebook, toothbrush, cigarettes and lighter – but no sign of the owner's identity. Finally, Keith finds a wallet with money, credit cards and a driver's licence in one of the outer pockets. –
One night Keith is woken up by the distant sound of music somewhere in the house; he discerns "men in chanted prayer, voices in chorus in praise of God. *Allah-uu Allah-uu Allah-uu*" (p. 47).

Chapter 5

Keith is on his way through Central Park to return the briefcase to its owner. He hesitates, is about to turn back or get rid of the briefcase, but then he walks on to a building off Amsterdam Avenue, where the woman lives. She turns out to be "a light-skinned black woman, his age or close, and gentle-seeming, and on the heavy side." (p. 64) At the beginning, they both behave akwardly, and after some polite exchange, which reveals that they worked for different companies in the tower, Keith wants to leave and almost takes the briefcase with him again. This seems to break the ice, and Keith sits down on the sofa, is served tea and biscuits, and they start talking. Florence Givens (that is the woman's name) gives a detailed account of where she was and what she did when the plane hit the tower and what happened after that on her way down the stairway. For the first time, the reader gets a full-length and very moving impression of what the situation in the towers might have been like after the terror attacks. Florence tells Keith about her surprise and shock, the injured men and women with whom she went the long way down the stairs through the dense smoke, always wondering what the reason for the disaster was. Keith realizes why his being there and listening is so important: "She wanted to tell him everything. This was clear to him. Maybe she'd forgotten he was there, in the tower, or maybe he was the one she needed to tell for precisely that reason. He knew she hadn't talked about this, not so intensely, to anyone else." (p. 69) Florence remembers the firemen racing upstairs and a blind man and his guide dog that helped her and others to stay calm on their way out: "[…] it was like something out of the Bible, she thought. […] They believed in the dog." (p. 72) There also was a maintenance man, whom Florence knew, with a crowbar, and Keith remembers having seen the man, too, which forms a kind of bond between them. More and more details come up and Keith listens to Florence's story with eager interest and personal involvement: "He listened carefully, noting every detail, trying to find himself in the crowd." (p. 73) –
Keith's life is in a state of limbo; most of the time he observes himself, things

he does and things around him. Nothing is routine any more: "Nothing seemed familiar, being here, in a family again, and he felt strange to himself, or always had, but it was different now because he was watching." (p. 82) He takes Justin to school or takes him home again, something he enjoys. As a kind of game from school, the boy has to speak in monosyllables, carefully watching every word and counting the syllables. This corresponds with Keith's careful way of watching and reflecting on life: "It was Keith as well who was going slow, easing inward." (p. 83) He thinks about minor details, in incoherent ways; sometimes he only takes in the things he sees without thinking much at all. There is a hint that he goes to see Florence: "[…] and there was the woman who lived across the park. But that was another matter, the walk across the park." (p. 84)

Lianne remembers her mother's warning not to marry Keith as Nina thought him to be a man reliable and loyal only to male friends, " 'but sheer hell on women' " (p. 74). Lianne now observes the present-day Keith, "a man she'd never known before." (p. 75) He still seems somewhat strange, doing his wrist exercises, spending time with Justin, and obviously enjoying it.
One day Lianne goes to see Dr. Apter, who is in charge of the Alzheimer patients, to discuss the members of the writing group and the results of the writing. She wants to increase the frequency of the meetings, but the doctor rejects this; he does not want the patients to feel under pressure, but they should enjoy the writing like "sweet music" (ibid.). Finally he reminds Lianne that the writing group is meant to be for the patients and not for her.

In one of the meetings of the writing group, the Alzheimer patients write about the terror attacks, "the planes", where they were when the attacks happened and about people they know who were in or near the towers (cf. p. 76). Most of their writing and discussing afterwards circles around the question of God and why He could let this happen. The group members show different attitudes towards God and also write and speak about different aspects of the tragic event that they are interested in; it is not so much a discussion with one actually referring to the other, but rather an agitated cross talk, with Lianne all the while encouraging them. She has to think about Dr. Apter's comment, which "disturbed her because there was truth in it. She needed these people. It was possible that the group meant more to her than it did to the members." (p. 77) Lianne, too, engages in the idea of God. As usual, she has to think about her mother's (seemingly ambivalent) attitude towards the question: Nina speaks of religion as making people "compliant" and returning them to a "childlike state" (p. 78), but also inspiring beautiful works of music and art. The patients go on talking, but they neither write nor speak about the terrorists. Lianne wants to encourage them: "There has to be something you want to say, some feelings to express, nineteen men come here to kill us." (p. 80) Only when Anna, one of the more quiet patients, talks about an aquaintance, a fireman missing in one of the towers, and states her helplessness because there is nothing and nobody ready to blame, Lianne realizes her own feeling of revenge, "the small intimate wish, however useless in a hellstorm." (p. 81) Anna, however, expresses the uselessness of these feelings, as the terrorists are " 'a million miles outside your life' " (ibid.), and they are dead. In the end, Lianne tells herself that, at present, she does not want to accept God's existence, although it seems possible (and many people have done it) to doubt and believe simultaneously. She feels that believing might make her weak, which she cannot bear in her present state: "She wanted this only, to snuff out the pulse of the shaky faith she'd held for much of her life." (p. 82)

In a scene in her bedroom, two weeks after the attacks, Lianne lies awake, her thoughts in a turmoil. Her mind is wandering back and forth between memories of her father, impressions of her everyday life with Keith, still in "transition" and not completely decipherable (cf. p. 84), her fixation on the newspaper stories about the terror attacks and the victims and her growing feelings of anger towards their fellow tenant Elena, a woman downstairs, who repeatedly plays loud, Middle Eastern or African music. Lianne is almost working herself up into a fury and decides to go down soon to confront her neighbour: "Ask her why she's playing this particular music at this highly sensitive time." (p. 86) In-between, memories of her past, especially the thoughts of her father and his stance on religion, calm Lianne down, just as her watching Keith, who is lying next to her sleeping, and with whom she has made love before: "It was the tenderest sex she'd known with him." (p. 88) She thinks about the word "husband" that she has never used for Keith, but now finds more and more adequate. Still, before she finally falls asleep, her restless mind returns to her uneasiness and anger about Elena's music: "All right the music is beautiful but why now, what's the particular point of this" (p. 89).

After one of her early morning runs, Lianne meets Keith, who is having breakfast in the kitchen. He teases her about her running, when the mentioning of Justin, who is in his room doing some drawing, suddenly reminds Lianne of a more serious matter: She asks Keith if he knows why Justin takes the binoculars with him to the Siblings. From a conversation he seems to have had with his son before, Keith knows that the three children have been searching the skies for more planes and that the girl, Katie, claims she saw the plane that hit the first tower flying by from the window of their flat on the twenty-seventh floor. Lianne is scared by the children's "'goddam twisted powers of imagination'" (p. 91), and the two of them speak about Justin's refusal to admit that the towers came down, although both Lianne and Keith told him they did. Neither does he want to speak about the fact that his father was in one of the towers when it was hit. The question of the name Bill Lawton crosses Lianne's mind, and again Keith is able to contribute at least a few pieces of information from a conversation with Justin, although he has promised not to tell anyone. It seems that Robert, Katie's little brother, created the name Bill Lawton when he overheard people on TV or at school talking about (Osama) bin Laden. Since then, the name has remained with the three children's own private myth of the leading terrorist and his frightening abilities and intentions: "'Bill Lawton has a long beard. He wears a long robe [...] He flies jet planes and speaks thirteen languages but not English except to his wives. What else? He has the power to poison what we eat but only certain foods. They're working on the list.'" (p. 94) Lianne gets angry about this "childish" way of dealing with the events: "'They killed your best friend. They are fucking outright murderers. Two friends, two friends.'" (ibid.) Finally, Lianne wants to know if Keith plans to stay and if they should not talk about it. Keith, however, thinks that they talked too much in the past and that all that discussing and arguing killed their relationship. They come to a very cautious conclusion regarding their present situation:

> "'All right. But is it possible? Here's my question,' she said. 'Is it possible you and I are done with conflict? You know what I mean. The everyday friction. The every-word-every-breath schedule we were on before we split. Is it possible this is over? We don't need this anymore. We can live without it. Am I right?'
> 'We're ready to sink into our little lives,' he said." (p. 95)

On Marienstrasse

For the first time in the story, there is a complete change in setting, characters and narrative perspective. The reader gets to know **Hammad**, a young Arabic student in Hamburg. The point of time, as can only gradually be deduced in the course of the narrative, must be some two or three years before the 9/11 terror attacks. Several scenes show Hammad's everyday life, his contact with radical fellow students and his slow development into a fanatic Islamist.

At the beginning, Hammad is standing in front of the mosque that he goes to, talking to an older man who was a soldier in Saddam's army during the Iran-Iraq War in the 1980s and now lives in Hamburg, working as a baker. The man tells Hammad how he had to kill young boys who were used as a kind of cannon fodder in the military tactics of the Iranian Ayatollahs, and that he feels the power of this way of dying as martyrs: "Then he said he was twice regretful, first to see the boys die, sent out to explode land mines and to run under tanks and into walls of gunfire, and then to think they were winning, these children, defeating us in the manner of their dying." (p. 98)
Hammad belongs to a circle of Arabic students, who study architecture, engineering, or urban planning in Hamburg. They live and meet in a flat on Marienstrasse, where they lead fervent discussions; each of them has started growing a beard. Hammad is particularly attracted to a fascinating young man called Amir; later we are told that his full name is Mohamed Mohamed el-Amir el-Sayed Atta (one of the very few references to the real terrorists of 9/11; see the chronology on pp. 9–10 of this study aid). Amir is the one who instils fanaticism in the others: "Islam is the struggle against the enemy, near enemy and far, Jews first, for all things unjust and hateful, and then the Americans." (p. 100) Together they watch videos of jihad in other countries, and Hammad is intimidated by the others' violent and ruthless attitude. But he begins to feel like a member of the conspirational group; as a kind of initiation he even takes part in the beating-up of a man.
Hammad has a love affair with Leyla, a young woman of German-Syrian background, who lives in a flat with another girl, a student of English. Hammad seems torn between two different worlds and lifestyles. On the one hand, he enjoys being together with a woman and even thinking of marriage and babies. On the other hand, he is drawn more and more closely to Amir, who detests this way of life and attacks Hammad: "What is the difference between you and all the others, outside our space?" (p. 105)
In the end, Hammad's outer and inner transformation and his radicalization are obvious; he has become one of the "followers of the Prophet":

> "The beard would look better if he trimmed it. But there were rules now and he was determined to follow them. His life had structure. Things were clearly defined. He was becoming one of them now, learning to look like them and think like them. This was inseparable from jihad. He prayed with them to be with them. They were becoming total brothers." (pp. 105–106)

Consequently, he gives up Leyla, knowing he will never see her again.

Part Two: Ernst Hechinger

Chapter 6

At the beginning of the chapter, there is a flashback to the moment on September 11 when Keith appeared on **Lianne's** doorstep after his escape from the north tower, covered in ash and blood. Lianne acted automatically, calling the doctor, calling 911, switching off the TV to spare Keith the images of the terror attack. She gave him water, carefully cleaned his hands, face and head, while he told her of a shirt he saw coming down out of the sky. Lianne realized all the blood could not have been Keith's but probably came from somebody else.

The state of the Alzheimer's patients in Lianne's writing group is deteriorating: "They approached what was impending, each of them, with a little space remaining, at this point, to stand and watch it happen." (p. 118) Rosellen cannot remember where she lives and loses her way, Benny has trouble getting his pants on in the morning, Omar gets off the subway at a completely wrong stop, Curtis is not able to put on his wristwatch and he writes and reads about it in the same dark and serious tone that he used before, writing about an event fifty years ago when he allegedly killed a man with a broken bottle in a bar fight.

Once, when Lianne and Keith are walking down the stairs and passing the door of the neighbour's flat with the loud music, Keith kicks the door hard. Lianne understands that he has done it not because he is angry, but wants to enact her feelings of anger and vexation and thus, indirectly, criticizes her for her continuous complaining. The music does not stop, but Keith's action serves as a kind of comic relief; they both have to laugh.

Lianne, Keith and Justin are having dinner together and discussing a skiing trip to Utah during school break. For a while Justin does not partake in the conversation, although his parents keep teasing him, among others with a remark about him speaking in monosyllables. Suddenly the boy announces that this was not a school thing, but " 'Bill Lawton talks in monosyllables.' " (p. 127) Lianne is shocked, Keith tries to appease Justin and to make him talk about Bill Lawton, but Justin refuses. Lianne realizes that the situation must be difficult for their son, not to know if his father can be trusted or if he is going to stay at all. In the end, Justin bursts out telling them parts of the children's secret: Bill Lawton says that more planes are going to come and this time, the towers will come down. Try as they might, Keith and Lianne cannot convince their son that the towers are down, and Lianne feels worried about this kind of fairy tale turned upside down:

> "His repositioning of events frightened her in an unaccountable way. He was making something better than it really was, the towers still standing, but the time reversal, the darkness of the final thrust, how better becomes worse, these were the elements of a failed fairy tale, eerie enough but without coherence." (p. 129)

She tries to return to the topic of Utah, but Justin turns silent again and even refuses to eat his fish.
In another flashback Lianne remembers the situation of their marriage shortly before they split up. Keith used to drink a lot and when he came home, he seemed to wait for Lianne's questions or reproach with a belligerent air around him, devoid of any conventional rules of behaviour. He was not far from uttering a single word or sentence that might have ended the situation and their relationship for ever.

There are incoherent glimpses of Lianne's and Keith's everyday life together and the way they deal with the events that brought them together again. Once they are going downtown in a taxi, kissing passionately and being observed by passers-by in the streets and the taxi-driver. Lianne still is not quite able to trust the situation, "*It's a movie*, she kept saying" (p. 134), she feels that she is going through a phase of reshaping her life and concepts after what has happened recently: "But then she might be wrong about what was ordinary. Maybe nothing was. Maybe there was a deep fold in the grain of things, the way things pass through the mind, the way time swings in the mind, which is the only place it meaningfully exists." (ibid.) Lianne asks Keith about the friends he has lost in the towers, Rumsey and Hovanis, and also about the third one whose name she can only remember with effort, Demetrius, who has been badly burned in the south tower. Keith speaks about them, but only in a factual way; Lianne tries hard to listen and ensure he knows that she is listening, "because listening is what would save them this time, keep them from falling into distortion and rancour." (p. 132) Only when she asks Keith about the briefcase and why it has gone and he answers that he has actually taken it to its owner, she falls back into her old habit of scrutinizing and weighing his words, in this case *actually*, as this is the word "he'd used so often, more or less superfluously, those earlier years, when he was lying to her, or baiting her, or even effecting some minor sleight." (p. 133) Lianne knows that there has always been a contrast between Keith's reticence and her wish to absorb other peoples' lives, thoughts, feelings completely, to identify with them: "Other people have truer lives." (ibid.) Keith's professional situation remains vague: There is a job offer from some Brazilian investors in New York, so he starts to listen to language tapes in Portuguese and practices the language a bit. Lianne goes on with her reading of newspaper profiles of the terror victims; she feels some kind of responsibility to do this, but is not sure about her underlying motives. There is a scene in their bedroom after their first love-making, when Keith is in the bathroom and Lianne enjoys pressing her naked body against the full-length mirror, "nearly collapsed against the cool surface, abandoning herself to it" (p. 134) and leaving the marks of her hot body on the mirror for Keith to see when he returns from the bathroom.

For the second time, **Keith** has gone to see Florence in her flat; there seems to be an inexplicable bond between them. Their conversation touches on many different subjects, for example Keith's failed attempts as an acting or sports student, the course of his marriage, Florence's visit to St. Paul's church in memory of the 9/11 victims, or her short failed marriage to an older man, who died in a car crash after they split up. They also speak about God; Florence is a believer, who states that we only have to obey the laws of God's universe (cf. p. 112) whereas Keith shows an indifferent attitude: " 'I don't even know what it means, to believe in God. I never think about it.' " (p. 113) Most of their talking, however, circles around their experiences in the tower – this is the true connection between them and the necessity to meet and talk:

> "[…] he understood that they could talk about these things only with each other, in minute and dullest detail, but it would never be dull or too detailed because it was inside them now and because he needed to hear what he'd lost in the tracings of memory. This was their pitch of delirium, the dazed reality they'd shared in the stairwells, the deep shafts of spiraling men and women." (p. 114)

When Keith says he has to leave, Florence seems to be disappointed, even angry, and he stays, realizing that he is attracted to her – not because of her looks (which are rather plain) but because he can talk with her about things that he cannot talk about with Lianne. Florence goes to her bedroom to change the music from some sentimental classical tune to a vivid Portuguese

piece, and Keith follows her; first he watches her dancing, trancelike, then – on her inviting look – he begins to take off his clothes.
A longish flashback presents the regular Wednesday poker nights at Keith's flat (with six members of different professions) as a kind of re-enacting and digesting of their everyday lives: "[…] these games were the funneled essence, the clear and intimate extract of their daytime initiatives." (p. 122) At first they played many different kinds of poker, but then they started to gradually reduce the variations until they finally played five-card stud only, the most restricted version. Now it was all a sheer hand-to-hand battle for power: "They used intuition and cold-war analysis. They used cunning and blind luck. […] There were elements of healthy challenge and outright mockery. There were elements of one's intent to shred the other's gauzy manhood." (ibid.) To support the purity of the game, the players also restricted other habits: There was no food any more, only very few drinks were allowed. "They liked creating a structure out of willful trivia" – all but one player, Terry Cheng, who called the others "shallow people leading giddy lives" (p. 123). The players were particularly fascinated by the story of four German friends who had played cards together for decades and, after they had all died, were buried in the configuration of their seats at the card table. The importance of the poker nights for the six men is mirrored in that fascination: "They loved this story. It was a beautiful story about friendship and the transcendent effects of unremarkable habit." (pp. 124–125) The restrictions continued, including the banning of sports talk, television and film titles, almost like a parallel game. Finally they gave up on those restrictions, one rule after the other was cancelled, but they felt a bit embarrassed about it, "they tried not to wonder what four other players would think of them, in this wallow of wild-man poker, tombstone to tombstone in Cologne." (p. 126)

Once, when Keith walks through Manhattan (presumably on his way to meet Florence), he sees a woman on a horse in the middle of the street, who is probably going to the bridle path in the park. First he cannot believe his eyes, for him the strange sight does not fit into the surroundings; this mirrors his experience of disintegration on the day the towers came down, "when the witness wonders what has happened to the meaning of things, to tree, street, stone, wind, simple words lost in the falling ash." (p. 130)
Twice or three times a day Keith does the exercises for his injured wrist – he continues doing them, even when the wrist is fine again. It seems to be important for him, absorbing his attention completely.

Keith is at Florence's place again; talking about the strange sight of riders in the middle of the city, they try to overcome the uneasiness they always feel at the beginning of each meeting. They also speak about their work prospects, Keith's possible new job with the Brazilian company and the impending move of Florence's company across the river to New Jersey. Florence is unhappy because she fears that their relationship will not outlast these changes. She makes it quite obvious to Keith how important he has become for her: "'You saved my life. Don't you know that?'" (p. 137) She tells him about the days after the attacks, how she could not leave the flat or see anybody and that she tried to phone a friend who is missing, probably dead. In that desperate situation Keith turned up – other than him, Florence believes in Providence: "'You ask yourself why you took the briefcase out of the building. That's why. So you could bring it here. So we could get to know each other. That's why you took it and that's why you brought it here, to keep me alive.'" (p. 138)

Chapter 7

The beginning of the chapter resumes one story line of chapter 4, with **Lianne** still being in her mother's flat with Nina and Martin; she has just turned away from Morandi's still life with kitchen objects that – in Lianne's and Martin's eyes – resemble the twin towers. Nina denies this; for her the painting must not be connected to modern architecture, but deals with something deeply human, mortality. Looking at the paintings, even looking at bare walls, will be Nina's last retreat, she says. Lianne's effort to take the conversation to a lighter level is quickly undermined by her mother, who continues her political argument with Martin about the terrorists and their aims. As opposed to her lover's opinion, Nina does not see any political or economic reason behind the attacks, but the force of spreading fanaticism, masked in the name of religion: "'How convenient it is to find a system of belief that justifies these feelings and these killings.'" (p. 141) For her, it is like a "viral infection" (ibid.), not a conflict resulting from historical injustice. Lianne only listens to her mother's and Martin's different arguments until Nina gives them all a break by smoking a cigarette and talking about her grandson Justin and his way of drawing and painting. When Martin goes to look at the exhibition of old passport photos on another wall in the flat, they start talking about travelling. Martin wants to go on a longer journey with Nina, for example to Cambodia, but Nina does not react to his suggestion. Instead, she reflects on Martin's own passport photo on the wall and the different ways to recognize and interpret the man in the picture: "'Your face is your life. But your face is also submerged in your life. That's why you don't see it. Only other people see it. And the camera of course.'" (p. 144) Nina and Lianne start to make fun of Martin and the piece of art he tries to make of himself. The conversation calms down, Nina is getting tired and Lianne thinks of going home to be with Keith when suddenly Martin restarts the argument, again seemingly defending the terrorists' motives. A phone call interrupts him, and when Nina then does not agree to his suggestion to go away for a holiday to see ruins, as they have their own ruins in New York, Martin leaves the apartment after having issued his last, very provocative statement:

> "'But that's why you built the towers, isn't it? Weren't the towers built as fantasies of wealth and power that would one day become fantasies of destruction? You build a thing like that so you can see it come down. The provocation is obvious. What other reason would there be to go so high and then double it, do it twice? It's a fantasy, so why not do it twice? You are saying, Here it is, bring it down.'" (p. 146)

One night Lianne enters their living-room where Keith is watching poker on TV without much interest, as it is not the real thing, and explaining parts of the game to Justin. Lianne is not interested in the game, but in the players, "they drew her in, deadpan, drowsy, slouched, men in misfortune" (p. 147). She makes a connection to the Danish philosopher Kierkegaard whose texts she loved to read during her time as a student and whose theories fascinated her and seem to fit to the situation of the poker players: "Wasn't there a soul struggle, a sense of continuing dilemma, even in the winner's little blink of winning?" (ibid.) While Keith is sitting there with a drink, obviously reconciled with his situation, and every once in a while directing Justin's attention to the game, Lianne's mind is wandering to the past. She remembers her situation as a student, when her mother sent her great books of fiction, but she liked to read in an old book by Kierkegaard, all the time trying to connect his writings to her own life and to find some kind of solace and self-assurance in them: "*The whole of existence frightens me*, he wrote. She saw herself in this sentence. He made her feel that her thrust into the world was not the slender melodrama she sometimes thought it was." (p. 149) Lianne feels good in the present situation, with Keith around and familiar sounds like a car alarm in the streets; finally she takes Justin to bed, who has vaguely agreed to his father's suggestion to get a set of poker chips and cards.

Lianne goes down to her neighbour Elena's apartment to complain about the loud Arabic-sounding music. Elena has a big black dog that joins them at the door when the tone of the conversation gets more and more aggressive. Lianne reproaches her neighbour for not being sensitive, playing that kind of music in the present circumstances: " 'The whole city is ultrasensitive right now. Where have you been hiding?' " (p. 151) Elena, however, emphasizes that it is just music: " 'Music, that's all. I like it. It's beautiful. It gives me peace. I like it, I play it.' " (p. 150) In the end they even get violent when Lianne puts her hand hard in Elena's face and Elena tries to hit her. Lianne realizes that she behaves in a rather crazy way and leaves.
An hour later, she discusses the incident with Keith, who calms her down by telling her she should forget about the music. Elena is still playing it anyway. Lianne insists she is not going to apologize. Keith mentions that Justin is afraid of the dog Marko, a Newfoundland. He tries to make fun of the situation, as for him " 'It's not a message or a lesson.' " (p. 157) Lianne admits to the foolishness of her behaviour, but explains it with her present state of agitation and lack of sleep. When Keith advises her to "take something", she refuses because she has had a history of taking pills, with bad effects: " 'They make me crazier. They make me stupid, make me forget.' " (ibid.)

With pity Lianne observes the decline of health of the different members in her Alzheimer writing group; especially the case of Carmen, who is not able any more to focus her writing on the task, but writes about her feelings in a highly erratic way, makes Lianne very sad. Once more it becomes obvious that the fate of the patients, Alzheimer's disease in general, evokes a great deal of fear in her: "Lianne herself, bearing her father's mark, the potential toll of plaque and twisted filaments, had to look at this woman and see the crime of it, the loss of memory, personality and identity, the lapse into eventual protein stupor." (p. 158) After all the patients have written and said something about "the planes" so far, they finally ask Lianne the important question: " 'Where were you when it happened?' " (p. 159) Lianne realizes that – after two years of working with the group and listening to their stories – she finally owes them a story herself. Thus she speaks to them of that terrible day, when Keith appeared at her flat and she took him to the hospital; she remembers many seemingly unimportant details. Lianne becomes aware of the importance of her telling for the group: "They were depending on her to make sense. They were waiting for words from her side of the line, where what is solid does not melt." (p. 160) Only when she talks about her fears of the future, especially of her worries about her son Justin, Lianne realizes that

the group is also very important for her personal way of coping with her present life: "Tell them everything, say everything. She needed them to listen." (p. 161)
In a flashback to her childhood and teenage years, Lianne remembers the nicknames she was given by her schoolmates as well as her father's visits in town every once in a while and his loving embraces. He stated her likeness to her mother in looks and character and told his daughter, who was fascinated by his liveliness and openness, the story when he and her mother first met in Greece and even the details of Lianne being conceived on Nina's second visit. He told her exactly the same details on the phone minutes or hours before he killed himself ten years later, when Lianne was twenty-two.

Lianne tells Keith about her father's suicide and his motive that she strongly believes in: " 'My father shot himself so I would never have to face the day when he failed to know who I was.' " (p. 165) The two of them are watching a news programme without sound, obviously a background story about the terror attacks with pictures from Afghanistan or Pakistan and fighter planes on carriers. At the same time their conversation passes on to Justin and his studies of birds he has to do for school and that they have to get him a book on birds. –
With a kind of dreadful fascination, Lianne repeatedly watches the images of the terror attacks on TV, not able to turn it off. These images leave a deep and indelible impression on her, "this was the footage that entered the body, that served to run beneath her skin, the fleeting sprint that carried lives and histories, theirs and hers, everyone's, into some other distance, out beyond the towers." (p. 169) Lianne sees the conflicting aspects of the situation, for example the contrast between the clear blue sky and the planes carrying terror and death, or between the victims crying to God and the killers acting in the name of God, too. Only once Keith watches the programme with her, taking her hand. For her, it is almost unbelievable to feel him and see the tower that he was in collapsing at the same time. They speak about their slow realization that this was not an accident, as they all wanted it to be first: " 'The second plane, by the time the second plane appears,' he said, 'we're all a little older and wiser.' " (p. 171)

A flashback gives the reader insight into **Keith's** life before the terror attacks and introduces his friend and colleague Rumsey, who worked with Keith in the north tower and with whom he spent a lot of his free time, playing hockey or walking around Manhanttan in their lunch breaks. Rumsey, who was a member of Keith's poker group, seems to have been quite a pathetic character in some ways; single, in a relationship with a married woman, balding, with strong compulsions. He had to count things, such as cars, windows, toes on women's sandalled feet, giving him a sense of stability: "Something holds, something stays in place." (p. 154) Rumsey was able to memorize (unwillingly) streams of facts and details that passed through his consciousness; only physical training, such as playing hockey, gave him a feeling of relief from his obsessions. Both Rumsey and Keith seemed confined in routines, with the odd outburst in a hockey fight. When Keith asked Rumsey once what he would do if he saw a woman with nine or eleven toes, his friend finally confessed what he was really looking for: He would ask her to marry him, " '[b]ecause I would understand that I was cured, like Lourdes, and could stop counting now.' " (pp. 155–156) –

Keith reflects on his present state of mind, his wishes. In contrast to the past, when he always wanted more of the world than he could get, without actually knowing what it was, he now wonders if his future situation might be similar to his father's, who is leading a lonely, contented life as a widower in Pennsylvania.

Memories of Keith's regular poker games: Terry Cheng was particularly skilful in dividing and stacking the chips on the table. He always payed attention to the stability and diversity in numbers and colours of the columns of chips; he never wanted them to look alike. The other players had complete confidence in him and never questioned what he did. After the planes, Keith has talked to Terry Cheng on the phone once, but there is nothing to say or discuss between them: "Poker was the one code they shared and that was over now." (p. 163)

Keith meets Florence at Macy's department store; she wants to buy a mattress. They also want to have lunch together before he has to pick up Justin from school and she has to go to a doctor's appointment. All around people, especially women, are lying down and trying out the mattresses – a rather funny sight. Keith suggests Florence do the same and after some hesitation she agrees and even makes a little show of it: "She bounced up, fell back, making a little game of her shyness in the midst of public intimacy." (p. 167) When Keith sees that two men are watching Florence and one makes a remark about her to his companion, he addresses the man with a strong invective. The man does not react at once and Keith suddenly gets angry and aggressive, he walks over and punches the man in the face. "Because if anyone said a harsh word to Florence, or raised a hand to Florence, or insulted her in any way, Keith was ready to kill him." (p. 168) Now the man attacks Keith, who hits him again – under the eyes of the other custumors they are quickly separated by salesmen and security guards.

Chapter 8

Keith's affair with Florence is going on; although they enjoy having sex, the most important reason to meet is still their common experience, "the timeless drift in the long spiral down" (p. 172). Florence has problems to cope with Keith's having to leave her each time they have been together, whereas Keith – who has lately thought of leading a more serious and responsible life – seems to be rather detached, as if he is watching himself as a different person, "ready to say what someone always says." (p. 173) –
In a fitness centre Keith watches men and women doing all kinds of physical training; for him, the atmosphere has a touch of sexuality, but there is more – he feels a kind of bond between him and these people, doing their demanding and exhausting exercises, "a spirit, a kinship of trust" (p. 180). Keith has obviously decided to take up a new job and wants to come to the fitness centre because he thinks that after work, he will need "an offsetting discipline, a form of controlled behavior, voluntary, that kept him from shambling into the house hating everybody." (ibid.)
Another short flashback to the weekly poker round with three men called by their last names, Dockery, Rumsey, Hovanis, and two by their first names, Demetrius and Keith; Terry Cheng always being Terry Cheng. One night one of the men told Rumsey that his whole life would be different if one letter in his name was different, an *a* for the *u*. The theory was that his life and character, for example his slowness and clumsiness, was determined by his name, Rumsey instead of Ramsey. The others watched Rumsey sitting still, as if having accepted his fate.

Lianne has been invited to lunch by Carol Shoup and expects a new assignment. Instead, she finds out that Carol has given the editing of her new publication to somebody else; it is an allegedly tedious and badly written book by a retired aeronautical engineer, predicting the terror attacks of 9/11. As a kind of apology, Carol mentions that she did not dare to ask Lianne to work on such a book in her specific situation. Lianne is furious because it would have meant quite a lot of money for a start; and the more Carol speaks about the book, the more Lianne feels that it would be exactly the work she would have liked to do: "The only book Carol mentioned was precisely the one not intended for Lianne and precisely the one that Lianne needed to edit." (pp. 175–176) Carol tries to distract Lianne by asking about Keith and their situation at home, but Lianne does not want to talk about it; she only mentions that she has hit a woman who made her angry. Carol is shocked and tells Lianne to show some happiness because of Keith being alive and back with her, but she cannot placate her. –

Rosellen, a member of the Alzheimer writing group, does no longer come to the meetings when she cannot remember where she lives. The others want to write about her, and while they are working, Lianne's mind is wandering off to the old passport photos in her mother's apartment. She sees members of the group in the same kind of setting, as if in the frozen moment of a photograph, and she starts to go beyond the surface of the photos she remembers and think about the possible lives and fates behind them. This gives her a sense of the importance of the past, people's histories. "Such beauty in faded lives, she thought, in images, words, languages, signatures, stamped advisories." (p. 179) At the same time she fears for the members of the group: "She knows they are not looking out of a tinted mist, as the passport bearers are, but receding into one" (ibid.); she is afraid of hearing what they have written about Rosellen, who has already faded away.

Picking up a thread from chapter 7, there is the continuation of the scene with Lianne in her mother's apartment after an angry Martin has left; Nina, drowsy from her medication, has fallen asleep and Lianne is in the kitchen to find something to eat. After Nina has woken up again and Lianne has reproached her for taking too many pills and stopping her physical therapy, they have a long conversation about Martin. Confused by his intense behaviour and argumentation some ten minutes ago, Lianne urgently questions her mother about her lover of twenty years. At first Nina is rather reserved about it and only makes vague allusions to Martin's past. It seems that Martin Ridnour is not his real name and that he was a kind of political activist before he and Nina met. It was Nina who introduced him to art and art dealing and she, too, set off his liking of the Italian painter Morandi, whom he had criticized before. Lianne suspects Martin's liking and interest of being purely materialistic, the more so when she learns that he used to deal in stolen art once. She continues to interview her mother, who gradually unveils more facts about Martin: He was a member of Kommune One, a collective demonstrating against the German state in the 1960s, and Nina thinks that he was also politically active in Italy at the time of the Red Brigades in the seventies. She emphasizes, however, that he did not belong to the German terrorists of the early seventies (presumably the Baader-Meinhof group) – he once showed

Nina a wanted poster with names and faces of nineteen terrorists, his face was not on it. The two women realize that there have also been nineteen terrorists in the attacks on 9/11 and Nina adds that Martin sees parallels: " 'He thinks they're all part of the same classical pattern. They have their theorists. They have their visions of world brotherhood.' " (p. 185) For Lianne, her mother's way of dealing with Martin's past is a weak spot that she is willing to attack. She intensifies her criticism, which makes Nina tell her a rather sentimental little episode of a snapshot on Martin's wall in his German flat, taken of him and Nina in Umbria at the very beginning of their relationship – and she finally confesses that his real name is Ernst Hechinger. Lianne keeps nagging her, for her the argument is only one facet of an underlying problem, the difficult relationship with her mother: "She wanted to punish her mother but not for Martin or not just for that. It was nearer and deeper and finally about one thing only. This is what everything was about, who they were, the fierce clasp, like hands bound in prayer, now and evermore." (p. 187) In the end, they calm down and speak about Lianne's present work, the editing of the book on ancient alphabets that Nina is very interested in.

When Lianne goes down to the basement of their house to do some laundry, she meets Elena, who is already in the small room waiting for the dryer to stop. The two women do not talk to each other, Lianne only hands Elena the dirty pan from Elena's washing to clean. Elena wordlessly bangs the pan against the wall she is leaning on and hands it back. After Lianne has filled the washer with her laundry they both keep their opposite positions in the small room, waiting, not looking at each other. It seems to be a continuation of their fight before: "There was no question that she [Lianne] would outwait the other woman." (p. 190) Lianne, however, asks herself what will happen next, if there might be any kind of interaction soon: "The question was whether a look would lead to words and then what." (p. 191)

Lianne walks over to the apartment of the Siblings to pick up Justin, who has spent some time playing with his two friends. After a cup of coffee with the mother, Isabel, she prepares to leave with an unwilling Justin. When Isabel is called to the phone in the kitchen, Lianne takes the opportunity to ask Katie, the girl, if they no longer watch the skies for more planes. Katie seems to enjoy being so important, but Lianne makes it very clear that the girl should stop the game, presumably because it frightens them all: " 'This is what I think. Maybe it's time for him to disappear. The man whose name we all know.' " (p. 193) And later, even more physically charging: " 'Maybe just maybe it's time to stop searching the skies, time to stop talking about the man I'm talking about. What do you think? Yes or no?' " (ibid.) Both Katie and her younger brother Robert are intimidated, and Justin clearly shows his mother on their walk home that he did not like her behaviour. All Lianne can think about is that she has forgotten the name of the terrorist leader (Bin Laden), thus again showing her constant preoccupation and fear of dementia: "It was an easy name, this much she knew, but the easy names were the ones that killed her." (p. 194)

Chapter 9

(The time in this chapter is, according to the very last sentence, "thirty-six days after the planes". There are only two different situations / lines of action, one with Lianne and the other with Keith, told alternately and chronologically, coming together in the end.)

Lianne is on her way back home after one of the sessions with her Alzheimer group. She is sad because she feels that the end of the sessions is going to come soon and she will not have the strength to start a new group. She thinks of Carol Shoup and desperately wants to have a phone message from her, telling Lianne that she can edit the book she wants. Walking west on 116th Street, seeing the elevated tracks of the commuter train, she comes to a building called Greater Highway Deliverance Temple. Lianne remembers that this must be the church where Rosellen S. from her writing group found shelter and help when she had lost her orientation not long ago. Again this triggers Lianne's fears: "This was an occasion that haunted Lianne, the breathless moment when things fall away, streets, names, all sense of direction and location, every fixed grid of memory." (p. 196)

Near the elevated tracks there is a schoolyard and a row of apartment buildings, the projects, i.e. council flats. Lianne, still deep in thought about Carol Shoup's possible phone call, realizes that something has changed: She sees faces in the windows of the apartment building, a woman is shouting, the children have stopped playing. Everybody is looking in the direction of the elevated tracks, to a point almost directly above Lianne. Then she sees a man in a suit, shirt and tie climbing on a maintenance platform above the rails, finally recognizing him (the Falling Man). "Why is he doing this, she thought." (p. 202) –
More and more people are watching the man, who has already fixed his safe-

ty harness to the rail of the platform. Lianne, however, is backing away, extremely unnerved by the situation: "This was too near and deep, too personal." (p. 206) While Falling Man is balancing on the rail, she asks herself why he has chosen this place for his performance, as he usually appears in places with big crowds. One woman shouts at him, threatens to call the police, some of the schoolkids even shout "Jump", but he does not move. Lianne thinks of his possible motive: He is waiting for a train, he is going to jump the moment a train passes and the passengers in the train can only see him jump or fall and, not realizing that he has a safety harness, will be shocked and excitedly tell their friends on the phone what they have just watched. "There was one thing for them to say, essentially. Someone falling. Falling man. She wondered if this was his intention, to spread the word this way, by cell phone, intimately, as in the towers and in the hijacked planes." (p. 208)

Finally a train comes and after some moments of intense concentration the man jumps and then keeps dangling upside down in midair in his well-known pose, very close to Lianne, who is both mystified and appalled: "There was something awful about the stylized pose, body and limbs, his signature stroke. But the worst of it was the stillness itself and her nearness to the man, her position there, with no one closer to him than she was." (p. 212) In Lianne, Falling Man has created a vision of Keith and his friends in the burning towers, that is why she cannot stop watching, but has to flee the place as she cannot bear the sight either. When she runs away, she passes an old homeless man, who has been watching, too, and seems totally frozen by the sight. Later she vaguely sees a police-car driving in the direction of the Falling Man, but she tries to ban the impressions from her mind. Only when she has reached a place uphill beyond the train tracks, all the time feeling her shoulder bag with the writings of the Alzheimer group knocking against her hip, Lianne finally stops her run and tries to calm down again. When she is standing at a street corner, much to her relief and joy she can see Keith and Justin in the distance, whose attempt to catch her on her way home has been successful:

> "[…] she saw them coming toward her, running. They were bright and undisguised, moving past people wedged in routine anonymity. The sky seemed so near. They were bright with urgent life, that's why they were running, and she raised a hand so they might see her in the mass of faces, thirty-six days after the planes." (p. 215)

Keith is on his way to pick up Justin from school. While he is talking to his son, his mind is occupied by thoughts of Florence, whose flat he left half an hour ago – never to return. He then told her that their relationship was ended. In that situation, they changed roles: He was the one who talked, asked her to understand, and she was the one who kept still, only her face showing her sadness and distress. Keith now realizes that he will be forty in about a hundred days, which makes him think of his father and his uncles at that age and of his own role: "How is it possible that he was about to become someone of clear and distinct definition, husband and father, finally, occupying a room in three dimensions in the manner of his parents?" (p. 198) All the time he keeps talking to Justin, telling him that they want to try to intercept Lianne on her way home from the meeting with her writing group.

Justin, who seems to be in a state of child's rebellion, is still practising his game of speaking in monosyllables. Keith, silently annoyed by his son's behaviour, pretends that he does not care, but tells his son to stop it because it upsets his mother. In a long reflection, Keith then decides to tell his wife about Florence and goes through a lot of possible and different reactions by Lianne, ranging from distress and depression to complete inner and outer withdrawal to the wish to kill him or throw him out and call a lawyer, presumably seeking a divorce. –
Keith and Justin are walking on, no sign of Lianne yet, and discussing if she might have taken a taxi or the subway. Justin, in "the mood of somber opposition" (p. 209), is lagging behind, giving his father the chance to go on thinking about Florence and Lianne. In a way, Keith is already trying to get the affair straight for himself, rather than for Lianne, when he processes reasons and motives in his mind:

> "It was not an affair. There was sex, yes, but no romance. There was emotion, yes, but generated by external conditions he could not control. […] He would say that the time he'd spent with Florence was already beginning to seem an aberration – that was the word. It was the kind of thing, he'd say, that a person looks back on with a sense of having entered something that was, in truth, unreal, and he was already feeling this and knowing this." (p. 210)

Keith behaves like a lawyer defending himself. Finally, he sees Lianne in the distance, at a street crossing, and he and Justin start running towards her.

In Nokomis

At the end of the second part of the book, we return to **Hammad**, who is in Nokomis, Florida, on the American Gulf Coast for the terrorists' flight training. The chapter displays both impressions of Hammad's everyday life in the States and memories of the time he spent in a training camp in Afghanistan, where he lost a lot of weight but gained a strong belief in the task that is waiting for them. In Florida, Hammad seems to blend perfectly into the surroundings and lifestyle of the people he detests so much: "The idea is to go unseen." (p. 218) The terrorists have rented a small house, they are careful, as they think the state is observing them. Amir, i.e. Mohamed Atta, receives money from Dubai; he still acts as a leader for the group, "Amir was electric, dripping fire from the eyes." (ibid.) Although Hammad behaves inconspicuously (he drives to the supermarket, wears leisurely Western clothes, often eats American junk food, likes watching TV from time to time), he is a detached observer of the people around him, the decadence and irreality of their lives. "This entire life, this world of lawns to water and hardware stacked on endless shelves, was total, forever, illusion." (p. 219) Fired by his memories of the camp in Afghanistan, where he once killed a camel with a long knife as a kind of initiation ritual, Hammad is getting more and more wound up in his hate and conviction to kill and die. "There was the claim of fate, that they were born to this. There was the claim of being chosen, out there, in the wind and sky of Islam. There was the statement that death made, the strongest claim of all, the highest jihad." (p. 222) Still, from time to time questions arise if a man must really kill to achieve something, to be somebody, to find his way – and: "What about the others, those who will die?" (p. 224) Again it is Amir who, in his fanatic and scornful way, dispels Hammad's doubts: "Amir said simply there are no others. The others exist only to the degree that they fill a role we have designed for them. This is their function as others. Those who will die have no claim to their lives outside the useful fact of their dying." (ibid.) Thus Hammad, like the others, even seems to look forward to dying soon, he again and again anticipates that day, "clear skies, light winds, when there is nothing left to think about." (p. 227)

Part Three: David Janiak

Chapter 10

Three years have passed (as the reader learns in the course of the chapter) and **Lianne** and Justin have joined a big demonstration with five hundred thousand people in Manhattan, presumably against the war in Iraq, "a march against the war, the president, the policies." (p. 231) Lianne feels detached from the situation and the scenery; this feeling is strengthened by a strange encounter with a black man who tells everybody that this is Charlie Parker's (the jazz musician's) birthday. Justin, who is now ten years old, collects leaflets handed to him by demonstrators, for example a woman in a black headscarf. It is for him, as a kind of political education, that Lianne takes part in the march: "She was here for the kid, to allow him to walk in the midst of dissent, to see and feel the argument against war and misrule." (p. 232) She tells him who Charlie Parker was and that she is going to look for some LPs at home to play for him. As it is very hot, Justin gets himself a drink, sits down at a building wall and starts reading a leaflet on *Islam*. Every once in a while, he reads a line in Arabic aloud from the leaflet or hands it to Lianne to read; this makes Lianne think of an episode some twenty years earlier, when she and a girl-friend travelled to Cairo as a present for their graduation. When they left the bus, they stepped right into the middle of a gigantic crowd that was celebrating the close of Ramadan, and the two girls were separated. Lianne vividly remembers her feelings then. Although the people around her behaved in a friendly way towards her, she sensed the deep contrast between her and the others, her existence as a white person: "She was privileged, detached, self-involved, white. It was there in her face, educated, unknowing, scared. She felt all the bitter truth that stereotypes contain." (p. 236) Lianne and Justin rejoin the march and shortly listen to somebody speaking to the crowd at Union Square, but then they go into a bookstore nearby. Here, "in the cool and calm" (p. 237), Lianne asks her son what the best thing is he has ever learned in school. At first, the boy evades the question with a remark about his father, who obviously is not present at home, but might be coming in eight or nine days, as Lianne says. Then he anwers: " 'The sun is a star.' " (p. 238) There is a bit of teasing between the two, while they are watching the end of the demonstration, and Lianne thinks how much she likes Justin's answer, thus showing her continuous circling around life and her place in it: "It seemed a revelation, a fresh way to think about being who we are, the purest way and only finally unfolding, a kind of mystical shiver, an awakening." (p. 239) They go home, and Lianne plays some of Charlie Parker's records from her father's collection for Justin. When he has gone to bed, she looks up Charlie Parker in an encyclopedia and finds out that it is, indeed, his birthday.

Lianne, who is still extremely scared of dementia as a kind of family heritage, does brain exercises, such as counting down from one hundred by sevens. She also undergoes a lot of tests, all of them telling her that everything is fine. "She was forty-one years old and within the limited protocols of the imaging process, pretty much everything seemed unremarkable." (p. 240) She continues with the exercises, especially the counting, as it gives her the feeling of order.
Four months ago, Nina died. Lianne, who does not go out very often and regrets this, misses her mother very much. She thinks of the memorial service with two of her mother's ex-colleagues and Martin, who flew in from somewhere in Europe. He had not seen Nina very often during the last two and a half years of her life, but Lianne had kept in touch with him, served as a kind of link between him and her mother. After the service, the four of them went out for lunch and Martin started a conversation about America and its role in the world. He was convinced that America would become completely irrelevant and said, rather harshly: "'It is losing the center. It becomes the center of its own shit. This is the only center it occupies.'" (p. 245) This kind of discussion was not seen apt to the situation by the others, but Martin did not care. Even when one of Nina's colleagues told him that Europe still focused on America, its movies, books, music, language, Martin did not give in: "'I don't know this America anymore. I don't recognize it,' he said. 'There's an empty space where America used to be.'" (p. 247) The colleagues left, Lianne stayed with Martin for a while, talking about Nina, his relationship to her, their long conversation that never stopped, even when they did not see each other anymore. When Lianne and Martin parted, she knew she would never see him again.

Keith is sitting in the Race & Sports Book in the old casino (Las Vegas) at eight o'clock in the morning; he can see five TV screens showing horse races and a few people around him absorbed in various activities, such as reading or intently watching the races. Keith still knows the time and day of week, but he wonders "when such scraps of data would become to feel disposable." (p. 242) Later Keith gets up and goes to the poker room, where he sits down for a tournament. Here, too, he observes some of the other players, when the tournament goes on endlessly; for him, they seem to find some kind of life and meaning in the game that he himself cannot yet see. All he feels is there is nothing else but playing poker that is of interest for him for the time being: "This was never over. That was the point. There was nothing outside the game but faded space." (pp. 242–243)

Chapter 11

After some months, **Keith's** life in Las Vegas has developed into a kind of routine, he is getting more and more successful at poker and every now and then he goes home to see Lianne and Justin, playing his role as husband and father, but unable to talk: "There was no language, it seemed, to tell them how he spent his days and nights." (p. 251) One day he happens to see Terry Cheng, a member of the old poker group at his apartment, in one of the casinos. The next day, they meet and exchange a few remarks about how they spend their time in Las Vegas, Terry also telling Keith that he has already spotted him before. They do not make any specific plans to meet again: "The idea of later was elusive." (p. 255)
Some time later, however, the two men are sitting in a hotel lounge for snacks and drinks; the world outside the poker scenery (for example the war in Iraq) is only on the periphery of their consciousness. Instead, Terry Cheng tries to convince Keith to join him in a private, "underground" poker game with well-off people and high sums of money in cities like Dallas or Los Angeles. Keith remains noncommittal, he thinks of Terry's position in the old poker group and generally in life, his being inflexibly fitted in the poker scenery – a feeling that appeals to Keith, this "crucial anonymity of these days and weeks, the mingling of countless lives that had no stories attached." (p. 260) Despite their being absorbed in their present situation, the two men also speak about the past, especially about Rumsey. Terry, who has never been so "talkative", tells Keith where he was when the planes hit the towers and what he learnt about Rumsey's mother, who again and again went to a building of the army with private objects from her son's apartment to help find a DNA match. Terry also says that Rumsey allegedly went out of a window of the tower after the attack; Keith remains quiet, but seems distressed, supposedly because he knows what happened with Rumsey: "Keith looked into the waterfall. This was better than closing his eyes. If he closed his eyes, he'd see something." (p. 261) Quickly the conversation returns to poker and some people they use to meet at the tables.

Once Keith happens to catch some news on the radion about a terrorist attack somewhere in Russia, where school children were taken hostages, and many died in a big explosion. Keith calls Lianne in New York, who is very upset about the terrorists deliberately choosing a school for their suicide attack. Although Keith realizes his wife's worries, the edge in her voice, he remains strangely detached from her and the situation.
Keith misses his son, though, both of them do not know how to talk on the phone. Keith regularly talks with Lianne instead, sometimes feeling so physically close to her that he cannot bear it.

We get glimpses of **Lianne's** and Justin's life together, it is not so easy for her to deal with her teenage son. One day, when she asks Justin if he has seen her nice silver pen, he does not answer, but his face tells her that he has probably taken it and lost or sold it. They have a fruitless discussion about pens, ballpoints and pencils; in-between Justin asks his mother about Keith. Lianne tells him that his father is going to go to Paris for a big poker competition and that she might go there, too. Justin knows that she will not be going; when asked about the pen again, he even insists that Keith has taken it. It is like a silent fight between them: "He was still standing, bread in hand, and would not look at her. He said, 'I really, honestly think he took it.'" (p. 257)

Lianne still goes to doctors regularly and tells Keith on the phone that the findings are "unremarkable" (p. 263). She likes the word and derives a feeling of security and relief from it. Still, she does not completely believe in the results of the tests and the doctors' reassurance, whereas Keith more or less reproaches her for her attitude: "He'd told her many times and told her again that she was devising ways to be afraid." (ibid.) Lianne, slightly drunk, speaks about her father again, then about Keith's father – and finally she starts reciting her brain training of counting backwards by sevens.

Chapter 12

Lianne goes to an art gallery in an old industrial building in Chelsea to see an exhibition of Morandi paintings and drawings; it painfully reminds her of the past, her mother, Martin and their arguments. When Nina and her lover first became estranged, she had Lianne send the Morandi paintings and the collection of old passport photos back to Martin, although both women regretted this. Now Lianne enjoys being on her own in the small gallery and looking intently at the small paintings on the wall, with memories coming back: "There was something hidden in the painting. Nina's living room was there, memory and motion. The objects in the paintings faded into the figures behind them, the woman smoking in the chair, the standing man." (p. 266) When a man comes into the gallery, the spell is broken; Lianne goes to the next room to see the drawings and then leaves the gallery, musing on the title of the paintings, *Natura morta*, the term for still life, as a mirror of her mother's last days.

On one of Keith's visits, he and Lianne have a long conversation about their situation. It takes them four days before they are able to talk "about things that mattered." (p. 269) Even at nights, when they are in bed together, Lianne reflects on the growing distance between them: "She was continuing to withdraw, but calmly, in control. He was self-sequestered, as always, but with a spatial measure now, one of air miles and cities, a dimension of literal distance between himself and others." (p. 270) They go to museums with Justin, and Lianne watches the boy and his father playing baseball in the park. Justin throws the ball very hard at his father, machine-like, relentlessly, although Keith tells him to calm down and ease up. Later Lianne watches a poker tournament on TV, while Keith is in the next room shifting through his mail. Lianne looks closely at the poker players on the screen, all the time waiting to see Keith at one of the tables. On the fourth day of that stay, they finally sit down and talk. Lianne, who does not really understand the fascination of the poker game, tries to explain to her husband how important his being around is for her and Justin: " 'This is the point I want to make, that we need to stay together, keep the family going. Just us, three of us, long-term, under the same roof, not every day of the year or every month but with the idea that we are permanent. Times like these, the family is necessary.' " (pp. 271–272) She also tells him that she is afraid of his drifting away from them completely. She thinks that he would like to kill somebody, and that he has been carrying this feeling with him for some time. Keith's answer shows that she might have a point: " 'Too bad I can't join the army. Too old, […] or I could kill without penalty and then come home and be a family.' " (p. 273) They both feel that most lives make no sense after what has happened in their city and country, and Lianne is deeply upset about her own losing control of her life, although it was not her, but Keith who was in the tower. She tries to tell him that his sheer presence has given her emotional security ever since. Keith promises her that he will not disappear, that he will always be back. He also reassures her that he is not going to lose any big amount of money at poker and thus risk their future, especially Justin's education, when she mentions that there will be some money coming in from selling her mother's apartment. Finally they return to the question of poker and if Keith is going to Paris for that tournament after all. It turns out that it will be a game in Atlantic City instead, and that it would not be convenient if Lianne came along. She would get depressive watching, she says, and that she is not sure what this game will make of Keith. He does not react, and Lianne finally realizes what defines the gap between them: "She wanted to be safe in the world and he did not." (p. 275)

When **Keith** is away in one of the casinos, he sometimes sits in the sports book and watches the TV screens, with horse races and baseball games, but he never bets on these events. He just likes the atmosphere, the sounds, the excitement of those who have bet and then the calm again. For him, the most important is the poker room, the only place to remain "the agent of free choice" (p. 268). Here he feels structure and logic in a game that he can control, even if there is sometimes a kind of "dream logic", when exactly the card he needs is sure to come. It all depends on him, on his own choice, and not on any other element outside his personality, for example "a horse running in the mud somewhere in New Jersey." (p. 269)

Chapter 13

Lianne has been addressed as a potential juror, with five hundred other people, by the United States District Court. She has filled in a questionnaire, not all of the questions answered truthfully. When a trial against an American woman comes up, a lawyer who is accused of aiding terrorists and being closely related to radical muslims, Lianne is not chosen as a juror. She does not follow the stories in the newspapers anymore, neither is she eager to edit the books on terrorism and related subjects that are offered to her. –
Memories of her father and his suicide nineteen years ago are still haunting her, as she frequently circles around the subject of remembering, keeping and passing on memories. Lianne thinks that grandparents are very important because they "are the ones with the deepest memories." (p. 277) Justin, however, has only one grandfather left (Keith's father), who is literally unreachable for the boy. She sees herself in a kind of middle position, with only one memory "inescapably secure" (p. 278), the day of her father's suicide, determining her whole life. He is not, as she likes to imagine, buried in an old, windy churchyard somewhere in New England, but in a big mausoleum complex outside Boston with hundreds of others.

One night, Lianne by chance reads the obituary of a man called David Janiak in an old newspaper, only slowly realizing that this was the performance artist Falling Man, who died at the age of 39. As Lianne cannot get hold of any other, more detailed article, she does an advanced search on her computer. There are lots of entries about David Janiak, many pictures of his different performances and reports on his life and actions. She even finds the results of a panel discussion titled "Falling Man as Heartless Exhibitionist or Brave New Chronicler of the Age of Terror" (p. 280). Lianne takes in every bit of information about Janiak, who studied acting and dramaturgy in Cambridge, Massachusetts, and Moscow. His falls and technical equipment are described in detail, also the fact that he made his performances unannounced and was charged, fined or warned afterwards. There is an intriguing remark by his brother Roman, who helped him with the preparations for the falls: "Plans for a final fall [...] did not include a safety harness." (p. 281) When Lianne comes across the dispute over the possible inspiration for David Janiak's performances, a famous photo of a man falling from the north tower on 9/11, she immediately remembers that photo and the impact it had on her on the day after the terror attacks. She recalls every single detail of the photo, its almost artistic composition, although it was taken by chance and without thinking: "Headlong, free fall, she thought, and this picture burned a hole in her mind and heart, dear God, he was a falling angel and his beauty was horrific." (p. 282) She goes on clicking through the different entries: reactions of other people, possible medical causes of his death, information that Janiak never gave any explanation and turned down invitations by several institutes to perform a fall as a kind of theatrical work of art. Lianne learns that Janiak reduced his performances early in 2003, only appeared in rather remote parts of the city and then stopped altogether. She vividly remembers the day when she saw him perform on the elevated tracks, near a school, although there is no photo of that act. It is not so much the man she remembers, "[t]he man eluded her" (p. 285), but her feelings on that day, details of people she met then, for example a teacher with a whistle and a schoolboy playing basketball.

Chapter 14

Keith's life is now completely shaped by his playing poker in Las Vegas; he feels that he "was never more himself than in these rooms" (p. 286). When he is not sitting at one of the tables, he walks over to the other game rooms for a superficial chat with the casino staff or women at the blackjack tables. His days and nights resemble each other so much that he momentarily reflects on this almost machine-like existence: “He wondered if he was becoming a self-operating mechanism, like a humanoid robot that understands two hundred voice commands, far-seeing, touch-sensitive but totally, rigidly controllable.” (p. 287) He has taken up going to a gym again for a workout at a rowing machine. One day he rents a car, drives into the desert and returns after dark. It is only when he looks down on the brightly lit city from a rise that he gets a sort of distance to the “strange” life he is leading. Often he thinks of Florence Givens, of their short time together, but in a very detached way, only faintly remembering their shared experiences in the burning tower. It turns out that he has never told Lianne about his affair with Florence. All that matters now is the game that gives Keith a feeling of identity. He tries to avoid talking to Terry Cheng, he is not interested in Terry’s new persona and change of character, “three years after the planes.” (p. 291) Keith is completely absorbed in the game; the only connection to his other life being the wrist exercises he still does, although they are not medically necessary anymore.

The wrist exercises have become a ritual for Keith, integrated with his daily, or rather nightly, routine. He does them in deep concentration, the full programme of the days when he had to do them three years ago because of his injury.

Once again **Lianne** has to think of her father, of his talking about “human existence” with friends in a house on the island of Nantucket, when Lianne was a girl. The topic is still important for Lianne and also for people around her, three of them (she knows) are studying the Koran. When she remembers the first sentence, *This Book is not to be doubted*, she reflects on her own doubts. She has started to go to a church in East Harlem, which she believes is the church that Rosellen, one of the Alzheimer patients, went to. Lianne misses her group and tries to find a trace of their time together in that church. She also has a sort of silent dispute with her father, who was a believer in the religious sense, whereas Lianne sees herself as an “infidel in current geopolitical parlance”. (p. 296). Still, she enjoys sitting in the church two or three times a week and going along with the rituals. She has also kept her running and wants to take part in the marathon some day, “long-distance running as spiritual effort.” (p. 297) She accepts Keith’s sporadic visits and also the fact that her hair is beginning to get grey, she still avoids the subway. Much of her thinking circles around the question of God and whether she will believe one day:

> "God would consume her. God would de-create her and she was too small and tame to resist. That's why she was resisting now. Because think about it. Because once you believe such a thing, God is, then how can you escape, how survive the power of it, is and was and ever shall be." (p. 299)

Lianne continues arguing with herself about the presence and importance of God, even when she is at mass, following the liturgy. Then one day, when she undresses, she experiences a vital moment of clarity and knowledge about herself and her future life: "She was ready to be alone, in reliable calm, she and the kid, the way they were before the planes appeared that day, silver crossing blue." (p. 301)

In the Hudson Corridor

Hammad is sitting in one of the planes heading towards the twin towers of the World Trade Center; the terrorists have already gained control of the plane and Hammad has been injured in the preceding fight. During the last minutes of his life he tries to calm down and say goodbye to a world that he no longer cares about. Suddenly he remembers the suicide brigades of young boys on the battlefields in the Shatt al Arab (a story he heard about in Hamburg) and these memories help him to feel strong for what is going to come soon and what his mind already has a clear image of although he cannot see anything outside the plane. A growing excitement in the cabin tells Hammad that the crash is imminent – and within one long paragraph, in the description of the plane hitting the north tower, the narrative perspective switches to Keith in that same tower, thus closely connecting the fates of these two men:

> "A bottle fell off the counter in the gallery, on the other side of the aisle, and he watched it roll this way and that, a water bottle, empty, making an arc one way and rolling back to the other, and he watched it spin more quickly and skitter across the floor an instant before the aircraft struck the tower, heat, then fuel, then fire, and a blast wave passed through the structure that sent Keith Neudecker out of his chair and into the wall." (p. 306)

From now on, the reader is inside the tower with **Keith**, who does not realize immediately what has happened. He feels the tower lean to one side and then swing back, he sees ceilings open and things fall through, injured and even dead people and many people move into the direction of the exits, presumably to walk down the stairs. Keith, however, moves in the opposite direction to the office of his poker friend Rumsey, who is sitting fixed in his chair with a horrible head injury, only barely alive. Keith talks to him and, as more and more objects come falling through gaps in the ceiling and Keith can even see people falling down outside the windows, he desperately tries to think of a way to get Rumsey out of the office. When suddenly a glass partition and wall behind Keith break, he feels that he is hurt in the face by glass splinters and he cannot use his left arm when he tries to grip Rumsey to carry him. Moments after he has lifted Rumsey, the man dies. Keith then makes his way towards the stairwell and starts to walk down, with thousands of other people, dreamlike, overwhelmed by the impressions around them, for example the sight of another man falling past the window. The passage down takes very long and people have to stop several times, they try to keep a regular line and not to leave anybody behind, such as an old man who has sat down because he cannot walk any further. A briefcase that a woman is said to have left behind is passed down the stairs and Keith takes it and keeps it. Firemen come rushing up and Keith hopes that they will bring Rumsey and others down. Finally they reach the ground level and hurry out of the building; only now can they see that both towers are burning. Soon the south tower collapses and an enormous wave of smoke and ash hits the people, who keep running away, Keith among them. He walks machine-like and is unable to integrate his impressions or understand his situation. There is only one sight that he particularly discerns in the chaos around him: "Then he saw a shirt come down out of the sky. He walked and saw it fall, arms waving like nothing in his life." (p. 316)

IV Analysis and Interpretation

1. Form, Structure and Temporal Order

The novel is divided into three parts with a number of chapters each, but it is far from being a narration in the traditional sense. Although the story is triggered off by the terror attacks on the USA on September 11, 2001, there is no full-length description of the actual event. Instead, the biggest part of the narration relates the effects of that day on a small number of people, thus presenting the 'what does it mean' rather than the 'what happened'.
The author has chosen a specific formal structure by disrupting his narrative and its temporal order; he has created an **anachronistic collage**, a series of film-like scenes and takes instead. There is no consistent perspective, but a frequent change between the perspectives of the main characters, Keith and Lianne Neudecker. Story lines are fragmented into paragraphs of extremely different lengths, conversations remain elliptical and at times enigmatic, situations of the present are interspersed with flashbacks and memories from different time levels in the past. This narrative structure mirrors the main quality of the characters' lives in the aftermath of the attacks: the predominant feeling of disconnection, uprootedness; everything, politically as well as personally, has to be questioned and rethought.
In the first two parts of the novel, these 'jumps' within the narration occur very frequently, sometimes up to eleven times within the longer chapters. In the third part the narrative flow seems to have calmed down a bit, the structure looks more solidified; chapter 13, for example, is told from Lianne's point of view only. As a whole, this corresponds with the development of the characters' lives that have taken on a more stable, unexcited look.

Only very few exact references help the reader to establish the main time frame of the three parts, the first part comprising about a week starting from September 11, the second up to five weeks (there is the expression "thirty-six days after the planes" at the end of this part) and the third going forward to the year 2004 ("[...] three years past, since that day in September", chapter 10). At the end of each part, there is a kind of coda, another story line told from the perspective of Hammad, one of the terrorists, the time being before the attacks of September 11. When we follow the different stages of Hammad's life in that period of time, from his days as a student in Hamburg, his time in a camp in Afghanistan (mentioned shortly), his stay in Florida for his flight training up to his last moments in one of the planes heading for the twin towers, we are getting continuously closer to and finally reaching the actual day. At the end of the novel, there is a time loop in the narration to just before the beginning, thus taking us right into September 11 from both sides, so to say. At the same time the author has closely connected the lives of terrorist (Hammad) and victim (Keith), when he switches from one perspective to the other right in the middle of one paragraph, even one sentence, and finishes the story on a highly dramatic note.

For all its fragmentation and discontinuities, the narrative structure also has some **thematic strings** that are running through all three parts and can even be seen as parallel patterns in some respects. There is Lianne's continuous, harassing fixation on her father's suicide and the question of losing one's memory, of mental health in general. It can be compared to Keith's fascination with the poker game, his compensation of the feeling of loss, when two of his poker friends are dead and one is badly injured. Lianne 'works' with her Alzheimer patients, as Keith 'works' with Florence, to go over the events of September 11 as well as the effects of that fatal day on their lives. Parallels and contrasts characterize the two couples in the book, all of them affected in different ways by the events. Keith and Lianne are drawn to each other again, but their relationship remains in limbo, as they never really talk and work things out; Nina and Martin argue intensely and sometimes furiously, they drift apart, but their deep, inner relationship is never really severed until Nina's death.

All three parts have a **heading**, a name; as a common feature, they all seem wrong at first, as they are not the names the persons are generally known by. "Bill Lawton" is the young children's mistaken version of Bin Laden, "Ernst Hechinger" is the former name of Nina's lover Martin Ridnour and "David Janiak" is the real name of the performing artist known as Falling Man. The names as headings represent three different stages of the impact of September 11 on the characters' lives. At first, the horror and threat are right within the family, even the children are affected. Then, the events are put in a somewhat wider frame, historically, politically, personally, including the European perspective. Finally, there is the artistic (and artificial) representation, the fight against the loss of memories and maybe against the wish to forget. In any case, all three names symbolize an important thematic and formal feature of the novel: ambiguity, the failure or at least difficulty of rational and clear understanding and interpretation.

2. Point of View

The author of a narrative text has various possibilities to present his story and thus influence or even direct the reader's attention and reactions, two of the most important aspects being the choice of narrator and point of view. The narrator, not to be mixed up with the author himself, is the voice that tells the story; most of the times he is also a character, i.e. part of the fictional world, and he appears either as a first-person or a third-person narrator. The point of view is the perspective from which the events and the characters are presented; it can be limited or unlimited. For a long time, the 'classic' narrator has been the third-person omniscient narrator, his perspective being unlimited: He is more or less outside or on the edge of the action, he moves freely in time and place, knows about all the characters, their thoughts and feelings – to sum up, he has complete control and understanding of the world he tells us about. In reference to the development of the 'modern' world, however, that commanding style of narration has been seen as more and more inadequate. With catchwords such as growing complexity of the modern age, pluralism, lack of fixed values, fragility or loss of identity in mind, the author of a narrative text often chooses the limited point of view of one (or sometimes more than one) character to present the story. In this way the third-person narrator only has access to the thoughts and feelings of that one character ("selective omniscience"). The reader must concede the subjectivity, maybe even unreliability of the narrator and his limited point of view. (A first-person narrator, of course, can always have only a limited point of view.)

In his novel *Falling Man* Don DeLillo has chosen **selective omniscience**, i.e. a third-person narrator who presents the main parts of the story through the eyes of the two main characters, Keith and Lianne, and an additive story line through the eyes of the Arab terrorist Hammad. This seems a very apt choice, as the author is particularly interested in the inner development of his characters in the wake of September 11, their conflicts, feelings, fears, memories, attitudes, rather than in an overall, comprehensive description of that day.
In the first two chapters, at the beginning of the novel, the perspective remains consistent with one character, Keith's in the first and Lianne's in the

second chapter. Thus the reader is familiarized with the main characters and also (in a comparably detailed manner) with the most important features that will influence their existence ever since. In the case of Keith, it is his going through the inferno of the collapsing twin towers, his narrow escape; for Lianne, it is the question how this day will affect her and her marriage, as well as her strained relationship and continuous quarrel with her mother. After those two introductory chapters, the perspectives change frequently; it is interesting to notice that, once Keith's and Lianne's story lines connect, the perspective remains Lianne's – this may indicate that her development is of highest interest in the book. All in all, the reader is hardly able to follow one story line for a longer period of time. In a way, he has to collect fragments to put together, if at all, a coherent picture of both Lianne and Keith. At the same time the splitting-up of the narrative perspective, the change from one inner perspective to the other, offers the opportunity to compare the thoughts and emotions of the two characters, maybe even their attitudes towards the same situation and problem, for example their marriage. Paradoxically, the reader gets a more comprehensive and more confusing image of the couple: Nothing is certain, the more we know, the less we understand.

The additional parts of the novel taking up Hammad's point of view have been judged quite differently by critics and readers, referring both to content and aesthetic value of the passages. Undoubtedly, Hammad's story told from his perspective alone is an attempt to present 'the other side' of the event, to make the motivation and character of the terrorists more tangible for the reader – and, in a way, more human.

Finally, there are the scenes with Lianne's mother Nina and her lover Martin. These passages are related from Lianne's point of view and the reader's impressions are strongly influenced by Lianne's attitude towards the two characters, especially her mother. Still, these parts contain some of the longest dialogues within the novel. In this way the author adds to the multi-perspectivity of the story, as he gives Nina and Martin the opportunity to argue in length about the topics of terrorism and America, for example – without the subjective and biased views of Lianne's perspective. In the end it is up to the reader to 'do the work', to decide whose side to take or whom to sympathize with.

3. Mode of Presentation

There are basically two modes of presentation, i.e. ways in which the author narrates the events of his story: **panoramic and scenic presentation**. In a longer narrative text you will normally find both ways. Panoramic presentation (also called "telling") enables the author to summarize a series of events, span long periods of time and relate the action in a condensed way. In scenic presentation (also called "showing"), the author takes his time to present the scenes and events, the thoughts and feelings that pass through the characters' minds, at length and in great detail, for example making use of dialogue, reported thought or interior monologue.

In *Falling Man* DeLillo employs a combination of both ways of presentation, with emphasis on the scenic mode, as he focuses on the internal development of his characters rather than the external chain of events. One event of the external action, however, the situation in the World Trade Center after the plane has hit the north tower, and Keith Neudecker's horrifying experiences on his way down the stairs and out of the building, is related in a very detailed way, acting time being almost identical with telling time. Here the scenic mode of presentation – as well as the position at the beginning and the end of the novel – highlights the scene and strongly emphasizes the impact of this experience on Keith in particular and all the others around him.
In most parts of the book the scenic mode prevails, when the narration follows Keith's and Lianne's reflections, often rendered in reported thought, i.e. reported speech in the past tense without an introductory expression such as 'he/she thought': "But what made her think of this, ethnic shampoo, in the middle of Third Avenue, which was a question probably not answerable in a book on ancient alphabets [...]" (p. 28); "Disbelief was the line of travel that led to clarity of thought and purpose. Or was this simply another form of superstition?" (p. 81) Sometimes interior monologue is employed, an even more direct and seemingly unrestrained form to present the characters' thoughts and feelings, normally in the present tense and first person (or second person, as if in a dialogue with oneself):

> "Do this. Knock on the door. Adopt a posture. Mention the noise as noise. Knock on the door, mention the noise, use the open pretense of civility and calm, the parody of fellow-tenant courtesy that every tenant sees as such, and gently mention the noise. But mention the noise only as noise. Knock on the door, mention the noise, adopt a posture of suave calm, openly phony, and do not allude to the underlying theme of a certain kind of music as a certain form

> of political and religious statement, now of all times. Work gradually into the language of aggrieved tenancy. Ask her if she rents or owns." (pp. 87–88)

Another important feature of the scenic narration is the dialogue, which is used with different functions, for example making the narration lively and authentic. The dialogues between Keith and Lianne mainly deal with the events of September 11 and how they affect their relationship at present and in the future. As these dialogues are rarely interrupted by remarks of the narrator, the reader receives an unfiltered version of the characters' utterances; he can compare them with their inner thoughts and feelings that he has learnt about in other contexts and may find correspondences or contradictions. The dialogues, or rather arguments, between Nina, Martin and Lianne serve as a kind of platform to go beyond the personal level and discuss the historical and political reasons for September 11 and the topic of terrorism in general. In any case, the dialogues are an additional element in the indirect or implicit characterization of the characters in the book.
Panoramic presentation is employed in the flashbacks and in the relatively short chapters with Hammad. It allows the author to skip longer periods of time and single out only the most important facts that explain a specific situation of the characters. It is then the result of these past events, the effect on the thinking and feeling at present, that is of interest and may be dwelled upon in more scenic detail.

4. Language and Style

The language of the novel strongly corresponds with its main themes and overall structure. In order to convey the enormity of the initial event of September 11 in its aftermath, i.e. in the shock and disorientation of the characters, DeLillo's writing refrains from great dramatic and artistic exercise or overwhelming sentimentality and turns to a rather quiet, sparing prose instead. Just as 'falling to pieces', fragmentation and re-building are major themes of the book, the language is often scattered and elliptical, too, conversations are clipped, reflections are obscure and disorienting, sentences are very often paratactical and only loosely connected. Deliberately vague pronoun references or the lack of introductory sentences in dialogues often make it difficult to find out who is speaking to whom.

The first chapter of the book is a good example of the author's style and use of language; here are the first sentences:

> "It was not a street anymore but a world, a time and space of falling ash and near night. He was walking north through rubble and mud and there were people running past holding towels to their faces or jackets over their heads. They had handkerchiefs pressed to their mouths. They had shoes in their hands, a woman with a shoe in each hand, running past him. They ran and fell, some of them, and there were people taking shelter under cars.
> The roar was still in the air, the buckling rumble of the fall. This was the world now." (p. 3)

In a row of main clauses, one sentence adding on another, but in a very lean and unpretentious way, the author creates the catastrophe anew, here and on the following pages. The description of sensory details (e.g. "roar", "rumble", "smoke and ash", "office paper [...] skimming, whipping past", "windows smashed and noises coming out", "the stink of fuel fire", "the steady rip of sirens", pp. 3–4) makes the reader see, hear, smell, taste, feel it.
At the same time small, almost surreal pieces turn up in the writing, which have an enigmatic, maybe also confusing effect on both characters and readers. In this case: "A shirt came down out of the high smoke, a shirt lifted and drifting in the scant light and then falling again, down toward the river." (p. 4) The importance of this impression is heightened into symbolic meaning, when it is repeated in the last sentences of the novel: "Then he saw a shirt come down out of the sky. He walked and saw it fall, arms waving like nothing in this life." (p. 316)
The last chapter, as a whole, complements the scenic presentation of the situation in one of the towers after the plane has hit; there is an increase in narrative detail and intensity, but the sober and almost factual tone, the discrepancy between the atrocity of the event and its stylistically detached presentation remain: "He [Keith] stood and looked at him [Rumsey] and the man opened his eyes and died. This is when he wondered what was happening here." (p. 311) And perhaps the most sublime expression of the novel, as far as different levels of meaning and their linguistic condensation are concerned: "The light drained dead away. Bright day gone." (p. 315)
Another noticeable feature of the language is the strict rationing or even complete avoidance of words from the 9/11 lexicon: This expression is never used, nor the expression "Ground Zero" or the names of President Bush or Mayor Guiliani. DeLillo uses "the towers" instead of "World Trade Center" – and when the actual name of that building turns up once, it seems totally out of place in a context that is dominated by personal insecurities and individual views on the events. The characters' reference to the day is not "September 11", but "the planes" and time is measured by "before" and "after the planes".

For all its seriousness, the writing sometimes also offers short, unexpected flashes of irony and dark humour, for example when Keith, after having left his bachelor's flat, thinks that "it might be hard to find a taxi at a time when every cabdriver in New York was named Muhammad" (p. 34), or when he later thinks of telling Lianne about his affair with Florence and, in his mind, goes through a long list of her possible reactions, ranging from "She would say [...] this is not an unforgivable offense" to "She would get a steak knife and kill him" (pp. 203–204). Another set piece of strange, almost surrealistic humour on the verge of slapstick is provided in the scene describing Keith's and Florence's looking for a new mattress at Macy's, the big department store. Keith watches other people try out the different beds and mattresses:

> "There were tentative women, bouncing once or twice, feet protruding from the end of the bed, and there were others, women who'd shed their coats and shoes, falling backwards to the mattress, the Posturepedic or the Beautyrest, and bouncing with abandon, first on one side of the bed, then the other, and he thought this was a remarkable thing to come upon, the mattress department at Macy's, and he looked across the aisle and they were bouncing there as well, another eight or nine women, one man, one child, testing for comfort and sculptural soundness, for back support and foam sensation." (p. 167)

Here the description creates and almost relaxed atmosphere, a feeling of 'normality' and oblivion, before relief is again 'shattered' by tension and aggression, as Keith attacks one of the men who seem to talk about Florence.

5. Setting

Most of the action of the novel takes place in Manhattan, New York City, where the main characters live and literally walk around. Quite a few clues, such as places and street names, give the reader a rough image of their whereabouts. There is, of course, the World Trade Center at the beginning and end of the novel, situated downtown in the Financial District; Keith's apartment, which he lived in during his separation from Lianne, is nearby. Lianne and Justin live in an uptown flat, presumably Upper East Side; Nina has an apartment near Fifth Avenue, in walking distance to the Metropolitan Museum. Central Park is mentioned frequently; Florence Givens, whose briefcase Keith rescued from the tower, lives in an apartment near Amsterdam Avenue, on the west side of the park. The writing group with Alzheimer patients that Lianne looks after meets in a community centre in East Harlem, way up in the north of Manhattan.

In addition to the impressive scenic presentation of the situation in and outside the collapsing towers in the first and last chapters, there is only one detailed description of the place that has been known as Ground Zero ever since: When Keith tries to get to his apartment within the fenced-off area, he is an eye-witness of the heavy rescue work and is able to see the remains of the towers, "the strands of bent filigree that were the last standing things, a skeletal remnant of the tower" (p. 30). The vividness and exactness of the description is possibly due to the fact that DeLillo had the chance to visit the site shortly after the disaster; there were several other people, some of them speaking about their impressions into their mobile phones and saying things like "Oh God, I'm standing here."
The reader learns very little about the interior of the different flats, it seems that they basically have to represent certain traits of the characters or their relationship. Keith's bachelor's apartment near Ground Zero is only memorable as the place where the weekly poker games with his friends took place, those being the only carefree moments for him during his separation. Once this ritual must end because of the death of two of his buddies in the towers, he leaves the flat behind, never to return. Some details of Lianne's and Keith's flat uptown, the bedroom, the kitchen table, the living-room with TV, only provide the background to the different stages of their coming together and coping with their new situation. Florence's flat is of no interest or importance to Keith, who walks there through Central Park several times, "without thinking much about the room where she'd be waiting or the bedroom down the hall" (p. 172). It is just the stage for their short, intense bond. Nina's apartment, well-designed and decorated with valuable objects of art, almost museum-like, does not only reflect its owner's character and preferences, but also seems to intimidate Lianne, who finds it "hard not to whisper in such a setting" (p. 10). Thus it is a perfect symbol of Nina's dominance and Lianne's feeling of inferiority.
In the third part of the novel the reader learns that Keith has taken up a life as a professional poker player and spends most of his time in Las Vegas, only sporadically paying a visit to his family in New York. He has literally put a great distance between them, he even feels the need to return to that city in the desert, once he is in New York. Keith leads a life in rooms: In the centre, there are the gambling rooms with the poker tables; when he wants to relax, he goes to the sports book to watch people bet on horses or other games, he wanders through the lobbies of the big hotels or goes to a gym; he sleeps in hotel rooms. The world outside, both literally and metaphorically, is completely shut out. In one of the occasional chats with Terry Cheng, for exam-

ple, the two men only briefly touch upon the subject of the war America is leading (or, rather, on its TV coverage), then leave it: " 'We're poker players.' " (p. 257) Las Vegas, that place of highest artificiality in barren, desert surroundings, is extremely apt to reflect Keith's existence of seclusion, sterility, tunnelled vision. Once he rents a car and takes a drive to the desert; when he returns after dark and overlooks the vast, brightly-lit city from a rise, he realizes for the first time that he is a part of it and "how strange a life he was living" (p. 288). But this is a fleeting impression of a detached observer, of no consequence: "In the thing itself, down close, [...] there was nothing that was not normal." (ibid.)
The flashbacks and the appendices with Hammad provide short glimpses of different sceneries. Lianne's memories of her visits to her father's place in New Hampshire, "in the woods", emphasize both her father's different lifestyle, natural, down-to-earth, and the literal and metaphorical distance between their lives and Lianne's wish to bridge the distance. The places where Hammad stays, Hamburg, Florida, the plane flying down the Hudson corridor, in short represent the different stages of his development: the slow shaping of the terrorist's mind in the secluded community of his Arab friends, the infiltration into the life of the enemy he despises and finally the fulfilment of his life's purpose.
To sum up, the author is more interested in the 'inner landscapes' of his characters, the spaces and movements between people, than in a consistently detailed description of the outer surroundings.

The narrating time of the novel roughly covers five to six years, from the years of conspiration before September 11, 2001 to the summer of 2004. With the flashbacks to Lianne's childhood and youth it reaches back more than twenty-five years. Exact references to time, however, are scarcely found. There is only one other event that can be dated precisely beside September 11: At the beginning of the third part of the book, Lianne and Justin take part in a big march for peace "with five hundred thousand others" (p. 231). Gathering all the clues from the text, one may conclude that this is most probably August 29, 2004. On that day, United for Peace and Justice, a coalition of more than 800 anti-war and social justice groups, organized a protest demonstration against the Iraq war and the policies of President Bush in New York City, preceding the 2004 Republican National Convention at Madison Square Garden from August 30 till September 2, where George W. Bush was nominated for re-election. It was one of the biggest demonstrations in New York City ever, estimates of crowd size ranging from 120,000 to over 500,000.

These dates, however, are not reflected on a broad historic range, but only in their importance for the private lives of the few characters in the novel. Again, the 'inner feeling' of time, the very subjective chronology of events is the most relevant.

6. Characters

6.1 Keith

At the beginning of the novel, Keith Neudecker is 39 years old; he works as a lawyer with a property company in the north tower of the World Trade Center in New York City. Separated from his wife Lianne and son Justin, he has been living in a small apartment, conveniently close to his place of work. We learn very little about his relatives, only that his father leads a quiet widower's life in western Pennsylvania and that Keith has several uncles. There is not a detailed description of his outward appearance either, except a very subjective reflection of his wife Lianne (shortly after their reunion):

> "He was tall, with cropped hair, and she thought he looked like army, like career military, still in shape and beginning to look seasoned, not in combat but in the pale rigors of this life, in separation perhaps, in living alone, being a father from a distance." (p. 20)

Corresponding with these thoughts, there are quite a few clues in the text that Keith is a 'physical' person, very 'body-conscious', with a trace of latent aggressiveness, rather than a man of words and psychological argument. His mother-in-law, Nina, calls him "reticent". There is no mention of friends or social activities except his colleague Rumsey and the weekly poker round, which took place in Keith's apartment during the time of his separation. Rumsey, with whom he spent his lunch breaks and did some sports after work, seems to be the closest possible to a friend. Rumsey's death in the World Trade Center is a shattering experience for the eye-witness Keith; memories of it turn up frequently in Keith's mind. The Wednesday poker games with five other men was also of great importance to Keith, as it seems to have been the only time when he could relax and forget about the strain of his bad conscience regarding his cut-off family ties. Keith's need of some kind of stabilizing ritual and friendship is reflected in his almost sentimental love of a story about four German friends who played cards together and were eventually buried in the position of their seats at the card table: "It was a beautiful story about friendship and the transcendent effects of unremarkable habit." (p. 124–125) Thus, the forced ending of the poker nights, the deaths of Rumsey and another one of the players, has a destabilizing effect on Keith's life.

The strongest and most extensive blow to Keith's existence is, of course, his experience in the north tower on September 11, his narrow escape from chaos and near-death. On an initial instinct, he appears at Lianne's and Justin's apartment and stays, maybe to counter the feeling of displacement and loss, to find a new centre and stability. From the beginning, Keith is wishing for physical presence (not necessarily sex), for quiet and a new everyday routine away from work, rather than feeling the need to talk and cope with the events on a psychological level. He takes Justin to school and back home, he goes for walks, he continues the exercises for his injured wrist, even when they are not necessary anymore – all this gradually giving him the possibility to actually watch himself, to see what he is doing and, perhaps, to make himself understood to himself and the people around him: "There was a contained elation in these times, a feeling that was nearly hidden, something he knew but only barely, a whisper of self-disclosure." (p. 83) At the same time he has problems to come to terms with his inner 'turmoil', to integrate the different fragments of memory, experience, impressions:

> "Now he finds himself drifting into spells of reflection, thinking not in clear units, hard and linked, but only absorbing what comes, drawing things out of time and memory and into some dim space that bears his collected experience. Or he stands and looks. He stands at the window and sees what's happening." (ibid.)

His reunion with Lianne is somewhat half-hearted. Although they even have sex again and Keith enjoys his being shielded from the world around him at the beginning and being a relaxed father for Justin, his motivation to return is never fully explained, nor are their problems in the past, the reasons for their separation, discussed or even eliminated. For Lianne, Keith remains enigmatic – the more she tries to get closer to the core of his experiences. Thus he seems to confirm a judgment made by Lianne's mother Nina in the past:

> " 'There's a certain man, an archetype, he's a model of dependability for his male friends, all the things a friend should be, an ally and confidant, lends money, gives advice, loyal and so on, but sheer hell on women. Living breathing hell. The closer a woman gets, the clearer it becomes to him that she is not one of his male friends. And the more awful it becomes for her. This is Keith.' " (pp. 73–74)

Keith is the one who does not ask, but react, and when Lianne one day tries to have him express some kind of commitment for a future life with his family, to start anew, his answer sounds almost ironic: " 'We're ready to sink into our little lives,' he said." (p. 95)
Despite his wife's eagerness to read, watch and learn everything about the terror attacks, Keith is not able or does not want to share his experiences in the tower with her. Only once they watch the TV footage of the attacks together and for a short moment, there is a kind of bond between them, as he takes her hand, but his way of speaking about those moments shows the detachment of somebody who has never been a part of the horrible event – and his inability to fully grasp its dimensions.
There are, however, indications that Keith needs to share his experiences – only it is not Lianne, but another woman who can help him for a short period of time. When he returns the briefcase he took out of the tower to its owner, Florence Givens, he does not leave after that polite gesture, but prolongs his visit, giving her – another survivor – the chance to go through her escape from the tower again in a vivid and detailed way. He talks very little himself, only watches her and listens carefully, but it is an active listening: In his own way, he relives those minutes in the stairwell himself again, thus entering into a silent dialogue with Florence: "She was going through it again and he was ready to listen again. He listened carefully, noting every detail, trying to find himself in the crowd." (p. 73) Keith's walks through Central Park to Florence's apartment, their talking, become another kind of ritual for him in the weeks after the terror attacks, the similarity of their situations, their uprootedness, uncertainty about jobs, openness of the future being the basis for their relationship. Their having sex almost seems like a 'by-product' of no great importance to Keith: "They took erotic pleasure from each other but this is not what sent him back there. It was what they knew together, in the timeless drift of the long spiral down" (p. 172). In this context, the scene at Macy's (Keith accompanies Florence, who wants to buy a new mattress) is of double significance. When Keith provokes and physically attacks a man of whom he thinks he has made an insulting remark about Florence, it shows the intense connection he feels with Florence at the time; it also proves the fragility of Keith's present state, his unbalanced attitude towards his surroundings, which can only be expressed by aggression: "He was angry now. The contact set him off and he wanted to keep going. He held his hands apart, palms up, like here I am, let's go. Because if anyone said a harsh word to Florence, or raised a hand to Florence, or insulted her in any way, Keith was ready to kill him." (p. 168)

Still, Keith ends the affair after a few weeks, he drifts away from Florence, as he keeps some final distance from Lianne. Although he tells himself that his leaving Florence is necessary to finally start his 'new' life as husband and father, he is not completely sure about the latter: "How is it possible that he was about to become someone of clear and distinct definition, husband and father, finally, occupying a room in three dimensions in the manner of his parents?" (p. 198) There is always an uneasines about his future prospect of leading a 'normal' life again, with a new job and family; this becomes obvious when he reflects on his reasons to go to a gym:

> "He would need to do serious gymwork once he started his job, days away now. It was no good spending eight hours at the office, ten hours, then go straight home. He would need to burn things off, test his body, direct himself inward, working on his strength, stamina, agility, sanity. He would need an offsetting discipline, a form of controlled behavior, voluntary, that kept him from shambling into the house hating everybody." (p. 180)

Lianne seems to feel Keith's inner tension and restlessness, his inability to lead the life of a 'family man', and she later tells him she thinks that he has always wanted to kill somebody. Keith does not argue her idea; on the contrary, he indirectly agrees to it when he says: " 'Too bad I can't join the army. Too old, [...] or I could kill without penalty and then come home and be a family.' " (p. 273)
This conversation takes place three years later, when Keith has already taken up a life as a professional poker player, spending most of his time in the casinos of Las Vegas and going to New York to see Lianne and Justin every once in a while. It seems that he took up a new job after September 11, but only for a short time, then completely dropped out of his proper profession. His emotional ties to other people are even looser now, although he often thinks of Florence and regularly talks to Lianne on the phone. He misses his son, though; and as he does not see or speak to Justin very often, he is surprised at his son's powerful, almost aggressive way of playing baseball with him. Keith reassures Lianne about their future, he tells her he will always be around, there will not be any problems with money, but when she tries to get closer to the core of his personality, for example his motivation to play poker, he withdraws again. In Lianne's opinion, there is one basic difference between them: "There was one final thing, too self-evident to need saying. She wanted to be safe in the world and he did not." (p. 275)
It may be a different kind of safety, but being a part of the poker circuit does give Keith a feeling of being settled. His days and nights have a structure, yet

time and space outside the casinos are suspended, "elusive". Instead, he seems to be completely absorbed by the game and its props, the rooms, tables, other players – and he finally seems close to the questions who he really is and where he belongs: "He was fitting into something that was made to his shape. He was never more himself than in these rooms" (p. 286). Keith does not want to relate to the people around him beyond the game, that is why he rejects Terry Cheng's offer to join him for private poker games, with drinks, small talk. He prefers the anonymity of the big casinos, "the mingling of countless lives that had no stories attached." (p. 260)
Keith's compulsive attitude towards the game is perhaps partly due to the memories of the Wednesday poker and his lost buddies, especially Rumsey. Yet he tries to suppress these memories and does not want to get too close with Terry Cheng, who was part of the round. He is also making money with the game, but again that is not the most important thing, as he expresses quite simply: "He wasn't playing for the money. He was playing for the chips." (p. 290) It is the nature of the game that forms the greatest part of his motivation. When playing poker (and, for example, in contrast to betting on a horse), Keith has the feeling of being in charge, of keeping control of his actions, annihilating ideas like luck or chance by showing a strong spiritual discipline. (As a parallel, he improves his physical discipline by going to the gym or doing his wrist exercises.) All the choices are his only. And thus finally, if sub-consciously, with his strength and will in the game, Keith may try to overcome the memories, the nightmares, the experiences of being a plaything in the deadly terrorists' game:

> "Nothing else pertained. Only this had binding force. He folded six more hands, then went all-in. Make them bleed. Make them spill their precious losers' blood.
> These were the days after and now the years, a thousand heaving dreams, the trapped man, the fixed limbs, the dream of paralysis, the gasping man, the dream of asphyxation, the dream of helplessness.
> A fresh deck rose to the tabletop.
> Fortune favors the brave." (pp. 293–294)

6.2 Lianne

Keith's 38-year-old wife Lianne has lived like a single mother for one and a half years before the proper action of the novel begins, having had the responsibility of raising her young son more or less on her own. (There is no sign of Keith seeing them regularly before the events of September 11.) Lianne works as a freelance editor for a large publishing house, whose executive editor, Carol Shoup, occasionally finds jobs for her and seems to be a kind of friend or, at least, good acquaintance. (She sends Lianne postcards from her holidays and knows about Lianne's private situation.)

As with Keith, we do not receive much information about Lianne's looks at present; as a child and young girl she was rather skinny and a bit clumsy, but grew into a very good-looking young woman, "darkish, […] with large eyes and wide mouth" (p. 164). Towards the end of the novel Lianne realizes that "gray […] was beginning to seep into her hair at the scalp" (p. 298), but she does not do anything about it.

Lianne is the only child of Jack Glenn, a former architect, and Nina Bartos, a former professor of art; her parents split up when she was still very young and she lived with her mother, only rarely seeing her father, either in his cabin in New Hampshire or on his few, short visits to New York. Her relationships with each parent have always been a dominant feature in Lianne's life; Jack and Nina represented two totally different lifestyles and attitudes towards their daughter. Lianne's present state of mind, her thoughts and feelings about herself, her fears and compulsions, cannot be understood without having a closer look at those two characters.

From Lianne's memories, presented in several flashbacks, the reader may put together an image of Lianne's father. Although originally being an architect, he seemed to prefer natural surroundings and landscapes to big cities: He lived and worked on a Greek island for some time where he met Lianne's mother. Later he retreated to New Hampshire, where he took Lianne into the woods or gave her a rifle to hold. He seemed to love her dearly and was proud of her and himself being the father of such a beautiful young woman. Lianne was fascinated by his way of living – although completely strange to her – and enjoyed being with him, being taken in his big arms as a child, being accepted, even loved the way she was. The most shaking event and ever-occurring memory, however, is her father's suicide when she was twenty-two, i.e. sixteen years ago. Jack killed himself with a hunting rifle because he was diagnosed with senile dementia and did not want to enter the final stages of that disease. Lianne has been watching herself ever since, convinced of carry-

ing the same genes and being doomed to the same kind of disease. Hence, she repeatedly undergoes medical tests and x-rays and does brain exercises, she realizes every little detail that might indicate a loss of memory (e.g. when she cannot remember a specific name). Hence, of course, her taking care of a writing group with Alzheimer patients, where she deals with the slow process of learning how to forget, so to say.
To call Lianne's relation to her mother a love-hate relationship is perhaps too strong a word and slightly beside the point, but it is ambiguous and, above all, extremely difficult. Lianne has always had the feeling of disappointing her mother, of not living up to Nina's expectations: Her studies have not been deep and scholarly enough, have not led to an academic career, she has married the wrong man, Keith, she takes a different attitude to Nina's illness and criticizes her mother for her way of dealing with it. Often Lianne gets the impression, and suffers from it, of not being taken seriously or even being deliberately overlooked by Nina: "She watched, Lianne did, feeling something familiar and a little painful, how Nina at a certain point began to consider her invisible." (pp. 57–58) In the political arguments with Martin, Lianne mainly keeps quiet, only watching and listening to her mother, who takes the lead in these discussions. It makes her feel and behave like a little child again. She finds it easier to speak with Martin alone, then she can even touch upon personal matters, show some interest, even curiosity about the nature of the older couple's relationship, which obviously serves as a kind of foil to reflect on the state of her own marriage. Despite all the difficulties, Lianne also feels a very strong bond with her mother, with whom she has shared her life and many experiences:

> "She [Nina] opened her eyes, finally, and the two women looked at each other. It was a sustained moment and Lianne did not know, could not have put into words what it was they were sharing. Or she knew but could not name the overlapping emotions. It was what there was between them, meaning every minute together and apart, what they'd known and felt and what would come next, in the minutes, days and years." (p. 61)

When Nina dies, Lianne has a true feeling of bereavement, as a cornerstone of her life (the talking, even the arguing) has been taken away; however, Nina remains a kind of spiritual presence for her: "Nina was all around her now but only in the meditative air, her face and breath, an attending presence somewhere near." (p. 244) When she speaks to Martin after the memorial service, she is eager to talk about her mother and reveals that, deep in her heart, she has always wanted to be like her and has never been able to understand, let alone cope with her parents' separation. Martin resumes: " 'You will always be a daughter, I think. First and always, this is what you are.' " (p. 248) This statement, the haunting memories of her father, the strained relationship with her mother – all these aspects represent the basic and most decisive trait of Lianne's character: her deep insecurity, her inability to know who she is, to establish an identity of her own.

It is not surprising then that the events of September 11 completely knock Lianne out of the balance she has tried hard to gain. From the moment Keith appears at her apartment, she, too, has to face a kind of private Ground Zero. Those acts of terrorism trouble her beyond the interest and affection of a survivor's relative; she reads all the stories about the terrorists and victims and repeatedly watches the TV footage of that day, unable to switch it off, as if that might enable her to understand, both rationally and emotionally, the enormity of the deed. The fragility of her composure becomes obvious when – after having 'functioned' in a graceful way for some time after Keith's return – she suddenly shows an outburst of anger and even violence towards her neighbour Elena, whose Arabic-sounding music makes her aggressive. Or, for that matter, when she meets the performing artist known as Falling Man for the second time: She is both fascinated and deterred by his performance in front of her, unable to take it for anything else than another media presentation, and runs away:

> "There was something awful about the stylized pose, body and limbs, his signature stroke. But the worst of it was the stillness itself and her nearness to the man, her position here, with no one closer to him than she was. She could have spoken to him but that was another plane of being, beyond reach." (p. 212)

On Lianne's long way to her true self (to put it a bit pompously) or, more specific, to a clear idea of her place in life when " 'most lives make no sense' " (p. 273), she often looks to others first. After their reunion she hopes to find stability and support from an allegedly changed Keith and keeps asking him for some sign of a lasting commitment to her and Justin. She desperately tries to understand him, his reasons to come back to her, and to avoid the kind of tormenting talk that has put their marriage in jeopardy before. In one of their conversations towards the end of the book she admits to the importance of his being around, of giving her strength when he should have been the one to show weakness: " 'You were stronger than I was. You helped me get here. I don't know what would have happened. [...] You were the one in the tower but I was the berserk.' " (ibid.)

In that context the Alzheimer writing group is perhaps more a therapy for

Lianne herself than for the patients. Dr. Apter notices as much when he tells her: " 'This is for them [...]. It's theirs [...]. Don't make it yours.' " (pp. 75–76) By accompanying the patients through the different stages of their disease Lianne in a way relives her father's experiences and fears and also anticipates her own personal doomed fate, which seems inevitable for her and is only temporarily mitigated by the "unremarkable" findings of her medical tests. At the same time the group finally gives her the opportunity to put her own experiences, feelings and fears into words when they urge her to write something herself about where she was when "it" happened. Now she is the centre of attention, the one who can give a feeling of stability: "They were depending on her to make sense. They were waiting for words from her side of the line, where what is solid does not melt." (p. 160) When Lianne meets Falling Man for the second time, a deeply unsettling moment for her, she keeps thinking of the patients' writings in her shoulder bag while running away and focuses on their names and faces. She collects the writings and fixes them in a binder at home.

After three years, Lianne's life still has its loose ends: With Keith being part-time husband and father only, her mother dead, the writing group finished and the subject of terrorism turning up again on several occasions, she is looking for some other kind of relief. She has made a habit of going to a church regularly, but her attitude towards God and believing remains difficult. She likes the atmosphere in the church, the celebration of mass, but cannot follow her father's example, who was a believer and made her think that "God infused time and space with pure being, made stars give light." (p. 296) Lianne has adopted the role of the Western intellectual, rational sceptic, "an infidel in current geopolitical parlance" (ibid.), as she remarks with a hint of self-irony, whose somewhat high-brow argumentation ends in the statement: "God is the voice that says, 'I am not here.' " (p. 301) Nevertheless she almost envies the strength and absolutism expressed in the first sentence of the Koran, *This Book is not to be doubted*, something she has also sensed in the radical resolve of the Islamist terrorists before.

At the end of the book, there seems to be a moment when Lianne finally is completely aware of herself, of her history and the shades of her identity, not only physically but also spiritually – almost like an epiphany (to remain in the context of religion and belief):

> "It was the body and everything it carried, inside and out, identity and memory and human heat. It wasn't even something she smelled so much as knew. It was something she'd always known. The child was in it, the girl who wanted to be other people, and obscure things she could not name. It was a small

> moment, already passing, the kind of moment that is always only seconds from forgetting." (ibid.)

This fleeting moment of realization and self-knowledge leads to a conclusion that leaves the reader with openness and different possibilities of interpretation from self-assertion to resignation, depending on his overall image of Lianne's development: "She was ready to be alone, in reliable calm, she and the kid, the way they were before the planes appeared that day, silver crossing blue." (ibid.)

6.3 Justin

Justin, Lianne's and Keith's seven-year-old son, has been living with his mother during his parents' separation. By chance, he was not at home when Keith showed up at their flat after his escape from the tower, but was staying at his grandmother's apartment and doing a puzzle with her. Lianne is thankful for that, as it would probably have been a double shock for him, to see his father again – and in the state Keith was in, "'Like gray soot head to toe, […] like smoke, standing there, with blood on his face and clothes.'" (p. 10) In his looks Justin resembles his father, at the same time he conveys an attitude of self-control that makes him very individual for his mother: "He had pale hair, his father's, and a certain somberness of body, a restraint, his own, that gave him an uncanny discipline in games, in physical play." (pp. 48–49) Justin likes to play baseball and practises with his father, once Keith is a part of the family again. To the great pleasure of his grandmother, the boy also does drawings (e.g. a portrait of her). As a kind of unusual hobby, he collects pencils, vintage and fashionable ones, and he sharpens them regularly in a serious and controlled way. Lianne thinks that this collecting is just a status symbol among children, but she likes to watch the procedure of her son sharpening the pencils, his obvious love of rituals. His best friends are the Siblings, Katie and her younger brother Robert, who live in a high-rise flat nearby.
Although Lianne prevented her son from watching TV, he knows about the events of September 11 and has been told by both his parents that the twin towers collapsed. Keith also told him that he was in one of the towers when it happened, but Justin obviously does not want to talk about it any further. Instead, he and the Siblings have constructed their own story (Keith calls it a "myth") about the day and its effects, the extent of which is only gradually revealed to his parents, as it is supposed to be a private secret between the children. Only when the Siblings' mother Isabel realizes that they are in the

room, doing something with binoculars (that Justin took away from his father), the adults try to find out what is going on. From the fragments of information Keith is able to retrieve from his unwilling son, it turns out that the children are watching the skies for more planes to come and continue their work of destruction. The younger of the Siblings, Robert, picked up the unfamiliar name Bin Laden and turned it into Bill Lawton. Although his clever sister Katie may have long found out the real name, they stick to the false one as another example of their secret code. The children have spun a complete tale around their mythical figure, thus indirectly expressing their awe and fear; Keith describes it to his wife: " 'Bill Lawton has a long beard. He wears a long robe [...]. He flies jet planes and speaks thirteen languages but not English except to his wives. What else? He has the power to poison what we eat but only certain foods. They're working on the list.' " (p. 94) This mixture of facts, half-truths and invented images clearly shows the influence of the omnipresent media presentation in those days – and the fact that the terrorist acts affected every single life, even that of small children.

Justin even takes an exercise from school, speaking in monosyllables (originally "designed to teach the children something about the structure of words and the discipline required to frame clear thoughts", p. 83) and makes it an integral part of the fairy tale. This becomes obvious when both Keith and Lianne again try to talk with their son about the events of September 11 and the children's reaction to them and Justin responds: " 'How do you know the monosyllables were really a school thing? Maybe not [...]. Because maybe it was Bill Lawton. Because maybe Bill Lawton talks in monosyllables.' " (p. 127) Despite his obvious lack of trust in his parents (especially his uncertainty about the future position of his father) the boy cannot help but give away parts of the secret myth, the most important points being that the planes will come back and this time the towers will really fall. Keith and Lianne try to convince their son that the towers have actually collapsed already, but Justin will not hear of it. It seems he and the other children are only able to cope with the events by repudiating the power of facts presented to them by the adults and instead reconstructing a completely new story about that day.

Justin's feeling of estrangement from his father or some kind of final reserve is never quite dissolved, even though Keith spends much time with him, taking him to school and back, plays baseball or explains poker (shown on TV). The boy's little child's rebellion, the distance he wants to lay between himself and the adults by way of body language and ritualistic monosyllabic talk, does not go unnoticed with Keith when they are on their way to intercept

Lianne after her writing class one day: "He noted the mood of somber opposition, the drag in the kid's gait. […] Justin pretended to lose interest, drifting toward the curb to study the dust and lesser debris. He didn't like being deprived of his monosyllabic powers." (pp. 209–210) Yet when they finally see Lianne on that occasion, the two of them, father and son, start running towards her, conveying an impression of happy togetherness, "bright with urgent life." (p. 215)

Three years later, Justin and his mother are more or less on their own again, with his father away in Las Vegas and having become such a fleeting presence that Lianne, half-humourously, wants to find him in a poker tournament on TV rather than the room next door, where Keith actually is at the moment. There is some indication that Justin suffers from the situation or at least resents his father's behaviour: When Lianne asks him once about a silver pen she misses, Justin, who has probably taken it himself, tries to put the blame on Keith, whom he does not even mention by name: " 'I think he took it. He might not even know he took it. I'm not blaming him. […] I really, honestly think he took it.' " (p. 257) And on one of Keith's occasional visits, when they play baseball in the park, Justin throws the ball in such a forceful, aggressive manner at his father that Keith is bewildered and tries to calm him down: "He told him he was burning a hole in his old man's hand." (p. 270)

On the whole, Justin has developed into a slightly difficult, maybe premature teenager, who seems to be interested in his surroundings (as can be seen during the peace demonstration when he collects leaflets and thoroughly reads them out to Lianne), goes his own way (no taking of mother's hand anymore!), tends to talk very little and in a laconic way, playing cool (" 'Yeah right' "). However, there is always a loving bond between him and Lianne, they are still able to connect on a level of carefree cross-talk: "They were enjoying this, a little tease and banter" (p. 238). Thus in the end, Justin seems to be safe in the newly found calm and balance of his mother.

6.4 Nina

Nina Bartos, Lianne's mother, is a retired academic, a former professor of art, who taught at universities in California and New York. Her age is not mentioned in the text, but as her retirement took place two years earlier, she may well be approaching seventy. This estimate is supported by the fact that she is ill: She had a knee replacement, she looks pale and thin and is on heavy medication, making her fall asleep frequently. The most important sign of old age, however, is her attitude towards it: "She was finally and resolutely old. This is what she wanted, it seemed, to be old and tired, to embrace old age, take up old age, surround herself with it." (p. 11) Most of the time she stays in her apartment not far from Fifth Avenue, her own little world, obviously designed to her wishes and likings, "with art on the walls, painstakingly spaced, and small bronze pieces on tables and bookshelves." (p. 10) Despite her growing immobility she sometimes walks the short distance to the Metropolitan Museum and spends hours looking at the paintings of the old masters, thus revealing perhaps her wish to be close to things she loves and has been dealing with for most of her life – and whose emotional and spiritual power and influence on people remains, regardless of insecurity and destruction all around.

As an acting character Nina only appears in the first two parts of the novel, in a story line presenting Lianne's visit to her flat shortly after the terror attacks, with Nina's lover Martin joining them, and when Lianne picks her up at Grand Central Station after her mother's quick return from a few days' holiday in Connecticut with Martin. She is, however, a continuous presence in her daughter's thoughts and memories, also after her death that is mentioned in the third part of the novel. Her dying seems to have been a longer period of suffering; Lianne tells Martin about it after the memorial service, "about the last hard months of her mother's life, ruptured blood vessels, loss of muscle control, the smeared speech and empty gaze" (p. 247), a sad and unworthy end for this strong, determined character.

Nina's influence on her daughter cannot be underrated (cf. 6.2). She is not happy about Lianne's reunion with Keith and – although she understands and partly shares her daughter's feelings in the stirring situation after the terror attacks and Keith's narrow escape – repeatedly warns her of renewing her marriage with that man. She has already made her final judgment about her son-in-law, whom she has never been able or willing to communicate with, holding him responsible for her daughter's instability and unhappiness – and loss of self-respect, should she stay with him in the future.

Apart from her role in the private sphere of the story (as an important factor of Lianne's development), Nina may also be seen in a wider social, even political context as somebody who is more or less directly affected by the events on September 11 and has her own, strict opinion about them; this is expressed exclusively in dialogues, arguments with Lianne and Martin. As a long-time resident of New York, she refuses to stay away from the city for long after the attacks, she wants to be in her home now more than ever. When Lianne asks her to leave, as many other people seemingly do, Nina stubbornly maintains that a 'true' New Yorker should be in his city now:

" 'Nobody's leaving,' her mother said. 'The ones who leave were never here.' " (p. 42) However, it is in the long argument with Martin, a few days after the attacks in her flat, with Lianne visiting, too, that Nina's thoughts, feelings, interpretations about the events and their background are clearly expressed. (This story line is split up into four different scenes in chapters 2, 4, 7 and 8.) Nina confesses that the images she saw of the falling towers have shattered her emotionally; but later she prefers to talk about the events in an analytic, argumentative, if agitated, style – with Martin as her counterpart. She does not accept any rational, political argument for the terrorists' actions, but says that they attack the Western world out of sheer panic. In a way she compares the terrorists (and all Islamist groups and societies for that) with angry children, who have not achieved what they have wanted from life and put the blame on the adults, not admitting their own faults and shortcomings: " 'Blame us. Blame us for their failures.' " (p. 59) Nina also rejects the terrorists' acting under false pretences; she accuses them of misusing the name and idea of God in order to justify their development into radicalism, hate, violence – a development that, for her, is not historically or economically justified but derives from a somewhat atavistic human urge:

> " 'It's what men feel. It's the thing that happens among men, the blood that happens when an idea begins to travel, whatever's behind it, whatever blind force or blunt force or violent need. How convenient it is to find a system of belief that justifies these feelings and these killings.' " (p. 141)

Sarcastically, she characterizes the paradoxical way of the terrorists' thinking and acting: " 'First they kill you, then you try to understand them. Maybe, eventually, you'll learn their names. But they have to kill you first.' " (ibid.) Despite their adversary roles in the argument, Nina obviously has a strong bond with Martin, her lover for about twenty years. Although she knows about his past activities in radical leftist European groups, she gives away only small and vague pieces of information to Lianne and repeatedly says: " 'I don't know' ". It seems that she does not want and does not need to know, as long as it is clear that he did not do anything comparable to those terrorist acts: " 'Look, if he'd done something serious, causing death or injury, do you think he'd be walking around today?' " (p. 185) Nina even admits to an emotional gesture: Martin seemingly keeps an old snapshot of him and Nina, taken the day after they had first met, hanging over his bed. She treats this with a bit of irony, calls it "maudlin", "pathetic", "[f]oolish" (p. 187) – but it is obviously an important symbol of their relationship for her.

6.5 Martin

Martin Ridnour, Nina's lover, originally German, works as an art dealer, dividing his time between Europe, where he seems to have several apartments and an office and maybe even a wife, and the United States. Lianne has never been sure about his true background and personal history, although she has known him for such a long time and always liked him. Martin is the only character in the book, whose outward appearance and behaviour are described in more detail (through Lianne's eyes):

> "Martin was overweight but did not appear ripe with good living. He was usually jet-lagged, more or less unwashed, in a well-worn suit, trying to resemble an old poet in exile, her mother said. He was not quite bald, with a shadow of gray bristle on his head and a beard that looked about two weeks old, mostly gray and never groomed." (p. 53)

Martin seems to play with his appearance, he enjoys being inconspicuous or not easily read, almost uninteresting: " 'This is me, I am shapeless' " (p. 52). However, from knowing him and seeing him together with her mother for about twenty years, Lianne realizes that this impression is wrong: "He was not the shapeless man he claimed to be or physically mimicked. He was unflinching in fact, and smart in his work, and gracious to her, and generous to her mother." (p. 57) After all, he (and not her daughter) is the equal partner with whom Nina wants to argue and start a political discussion about the terror attacks and their background.
In this argument, Martin takes the globally-thinking and anti-American perspective and thus strongly opposes Nina's position. For him, the terrorist acts result from a long history of political and economical inequality and injustice between the First and Third World: " 'One side has the capital, the labor, the technology, the armies, the agencies, the cities, the laws, the police and the prisons. The other side has a few men willing to die.' " (pp. 58–59) (These words may be seen as an expression of the concept that has been known as "asymmetrical warfare".) In Martin's eyes, the attacks on America are only representative of a more general fight against the dominance of Western values and Western materialism and immorality, and they express the wish of the Eastern world to be able to live decently according to their own beliefs, to have " 'their place in the world, their own global union, not ours.' " (p. 145) When Nina alludes to the devastating effects of the attacks, for example the ruins of the World Trade Center in New York, Martin focuses his criticism in a provocative statement that once again illustrates the extent of Western,

especially American, arrogance and hybris – the twin towers as "fantasies of wealth and power" that literally cry for destruction: " 'You are saying, Here it is, bring it down.' " (p. 146)
This somewhat sympathetic attitude corresponds with Martin's past, parts of which are gradually revealed to Lianne by Nina: His real name is Ernst Hechinger, in the 1970s he was loosely connected with terrorist movements in Italy and Germany, although not an active member. When he met Nina, he was just starting to go into the art business, sometimes even dealing in stolen art (as Nina suspects), and was influenced a lot by her knowledge and guidance. Since then he has been very successful, and the two of them travelled a lot; Nina has never felt the urge to press Martin with more questions about his past, which seems to have lost its relevance for him.
However, once that his political standing has come up in the argument with Nina, it makes the two of them drift apart in the following two and a half years preceding Nina's death. Their contact becomes less, only Lianne keeps the connection with sporadic e-mails and phone calls. She only sees Martin again at the memorial service for her dead mother. During lunch after the service, together with Lianne and two old friends of Nina's, Martin suddenly takes up that political argument again, showing clearly that his opinion of America has not changed: " 'For all the careless power of this country, let me say this, for all the danger it makes in the world, America is going to become irrelevant.'" (p. 245) (This is one of the very few indications in the book that might allude to what came after September 11, for example the United States' so-called war on terror and its effect on America's position in the world.) Again Martin pronounces the anti-American currents that have spread in the wake of America's dealing with the terror attacks and their alleged perpetrators and sympathizers: " 'Soon the day is coming when nobody has to think about America except for the danger it brings.' " (ibid.)
Thus, just like Nina, Martin is a character acting on two different levels, a private and a political one. The private Martin reveals his deep relationship with Nina; he knows about her importance for him and his development and maintains that this relationship has never been destroyed: " 'One day we started to talk and it never stopped, this conversation.' " (p. 248) That is why he obviously suffers a great deal from Nina's death and seems like someone "displaced or deeply distracted, lost in time." (p. 245) The political Martin represents the opposite attitude to Nina's as far as the judgment of the historic events is concerned, and in this respect the two of them are themselves only representatives of global systems of thinking.

6.6 Florence

Florence Givens is the owner of the briefcase that Keith took with him on his way out of the collapsing tower. After some days Keith finds out where she lives (near Central Park) and goes to her flat to return the briefcase. They establish a relationship, having sex, but mostly talking and spending time together. The affair is ended by Keith after a few weeks.
Keith describes her briefly as a "light-skinned black woman, his age or close, and gentle-seeming, and on the heavy side." (p. 64) Gradually he finds out that she also worked for a company in the north tower, one floor below his working place; they had never met before. She was married to an older man ten years earlier, but only for a short time. Her ex-husband died in a car crash after the divorce, and Florence was blamed by his mother – a mark that she cannot forget. It seems that there is some underlying sadness and depression in Florence, and she enjoys the moments in their conversations when Keith makes her laugh:

> "There was an element in Florence that was always close to some emotional distress, a memory of bearing injury or sustaining loss, possibly lifelong, and the laughter was a kind of shedding, a physical deliverance from old woe, dead skin, if only for a moment." (p. 113)

Within the story Florence, too, can be seen on two different levels, both being strongly related to the events of September 11.
First, just like Keith, she has been directly affected by the attacks, she is a victim that survived by lucky chance. Through her example, the reader gets to know a way of how people have tried to cope with the events: At first, she does not leave her flat, she keeps calling the number of a friend missing in the towers, but only at night so that nobody else could pick up the phone and perhaps tell her about the death of that friend. After a few days, she goes to a chapel near Ground Zero and sits silently, only watching people pray and reading the memory plates for the missing and dead. Obviously she feels the need to be near the place and the people who share her distress and shock. Only when Keith comes to her flat is she able to actually talk about the situation in the towers again and again, going, or rather living, through it in vivid detail and thus, perhaps, find a way to get over it some day and to accept that she is alive whereas so many others died. Being with Keith is very important for her, not as a lover but as a supporter who gives her the strength to face a future that is uncertain and that she would like to share with him. Hence her jealousy of his marriage, which will be the end of their story be-

ginning with the briefcase. For her the story must not have an end, the bond between them is irretrievable:

> "'You ask yourself why you took the briefcase out of the building. That's why. So you could bring it here. So we could get to know each other. That's why you brought it here, to keep me alive.'
> [...]
> 'You ask yourself what the story is that goes with the briefcase. I'm the story,' she said." (p. 138)

Secondly, Florence is another step in Keith's development after his experiences on September 11 (cf. 6.1). She is the only one that he can share his memories with – simply because she was there, too. Never a great talker, Keith does not mind speaking with Florence, not only about the towers, but also about his past and present situation. She seems to make it easy for him to focus and to open up, maybe because her insecurity (rather than Lianne's) is understandable for him – and even her strong belief in God (that he cannot share) is not a subject that puts him off (as in Lianne's case) but seems "unavoidable" and must be talked about. Florence (if only for a short time) enables him to give in to intimacy, both physical and mental, even if this relationship does not lead to a straightening-up of his way in the end; it remains an episode.

6.7 Hammad

Hammad, from whose perspective the three appendices to each part of the novel are told (only partly in the last chapter, as it contains Hammad's death), is one of the terrorists who direct the planes into the twin towers on September 11. When creating this character, the author has kept quite closely to the facts that have gradually been revealed about the history of the real terrorists in their last few years before the day of the attacks; he even has Mohamed Atta appear under the name of Amir in the story. As with the other characters, however, DeLillo is not so much interested in the outer chronology of the events (cf. pp. 9–10 in this study aid), in verifiable dates, but in the inner development of the individual, in this case from a politically uninvolved character to a man who is deeply and radically committed to a grave act of terrorism.
At the beginning ("On Marienstrasse"), Hammad is a student in Hamburg, probably of mechanical engineering. He goes to a mosque, but does not seem to be particularly religious. He has an affair with a German-Syrian student and sometimes even thinks of marrying and having children with her. The

flat on Marienstrasse, which Hammad is sharing with other students, gradually becomes a conspirational place for young fanatic Arabs, one of them being Amir (i.e. Mohamed Atta). At first Hammad is only a silent and intimidated listener during the meetings of the group and their fervent discussions about jihad and the fight against their enemies, the Jews and the Americans, but his fascination grows and he becomes more and more drawn to Amir, who does a kind of brain-washing with him and creates a totally new horizon: “This was Amir, his mind was in the upper skies, making sense of things, drawing things together.” (p. 102) Hammad starts growing a beard, too, and takes part in the beating-up of another man on the Reeperbahn, the reason being only vaguely known to him: “he wasn’t sure what this was all about, the guy paying an Albanian whore for sex or the guy not growing a beard.” (p. 103) Hammad realizes that his own lifestyle collides with the rules of the group, the believers, the “followers of the Prophets”, as they call themselves; Amir criticizes him in a harsh and sarcastic way for it. Finally Hammad makes a decision, or rather he lets the feeling of “becoming total brothers” (p. 106) with the others win over his old secular life; he leaves his girlfriend Leyla, knowing that she will soon be totally eradicated from his memory.
Some time later (“In Nokomis”) the conspiration has proceeded and so has Hammad’s development. The terrorists-to-be have left the stage of discussion and are now “in full and determined preparation” (p. 218). Hammad spent some time in a training camp in Afghanistan, where his loss of weight has been compensated by a gain of spiritual conviction, a strong determination to give up his life, to finally enter paradise: “[…] Hammad had begun to understand that death is stronger than life. […] There was no feeling like this ever in his life. He wore a bomb vest and knew he was a man now, finally, ready to close the distance to God.” (pp. 218–219) The group, led by Amir, is in Florida for flight training. Hammad is not very good at it (this is probably the reason why he does not fly a plane in the end but has to keep watch in the cabin), but he stubbornly tries to improve by memorizing the details from a big cardbord illustration in his room. Otherwise he represents the perfect embodiment of a conspirator, having completely given up any personal mark, his individuality, and thus going unnoticed in his surroundings. His single deviating thought, “What about the lives of the others he takes with him?” (p. 223), is quickly rejected by Amir, who succeeds in turning his contempt of the victims into a philosophy for Hammad. Hammad now appears tunnel-visioned, kept strong by his deep companionship with the others, his giving up of the “I” for the “we”: “This is our strength, to love death, to feel the claim of armed martyrdom.” (p. 226)

At the end, when he is sitting in the plane hijacked by the group, flying towards the World Trade Center ("In the Hudson Corridor"), he draws strength both from the memories of the boy soldiers in the Shatt al Arab, with their key to paradise around their necks (the story he heard in Hamburg some time ago), and from a kind of mantra that he silently recites to himself in anticipation of his death:

> "Recite the sacred words.
> Pull your clothes tightly about you.
> Fix your gaze.
> Carry your soul in your hand.
> [...]
> Every sin of your life is forgiven in the seconds to come.
> There is nothing between you and eternal life in the seconds to come.
> You are wishing for death and now it is here in the seconds to come."
> (p. 305)

6.8 Falling Man

The most unusual character in the book is the one named "Falling Man" in the media. He is not really acting within the story in a traditional sense of the word, but has two appearances, similar in structure, in the first two parts of the book; then – in the last part – the reader is subsequently supplied with more information about his identity, typically enough by an internet research of Lianne after his death. She is the only other character in the story who has witnessed his appearances and been strangely fascinated and deterred by them.

His real name is David Janiak, he is 39 years old when he dies "of natural causes", as the obituary says. Having studied acting and dramaturgy in Cambridge, Massachusetts, with a short stay in Moscow, he becomes famous for a single act: Shortly after the terror attacks on September 11, he starts to jump headfirst, in a suit and tie, from high buildings and structures, held only by a safety harness, thus enacting a well-known and highly disputed photograph of a man jumping from one of the burning towers to his death. As Janiak never announces his performances and always chooses public places with many people around, he always creates feelings of surprise and shock, anger and disgust among his involuntary audience. Ignoring all official warnings and fines, he repeats the performance in many different places all over New York.

There is no indication as to his motives or intentions; both Lianne's thoughts

when she watches him and the bits of personal details remain speculative, the character "eludes" understanding (as Lianne puts it).
Falling Man is gradually made into a piece of art, a topic for studied argumentation, for example in a panel discussion: "Falling Man as Heartless Exhibitionist or Brave New Chronicler of the Age of Terror" (p. 280). He is even invited to perform his fall in a museum or speak about it in cultural organizations – he becomes an accepted cultural asset. With this, Janiak seems to have lost the true basis of his performance and he more and more reduces his falls and evades to remoter parts of the city, then finally stops. There is some indication, brought up by his brother, who often helped him with the performances, that he might have planned a final fall without the safety harness. Even when David Janiak has not realized this plan in the end, all the falls before have done a great deal of damage to his health and – as he suffered from a heart ailment and high blood pressure – have helped to bring about his early death.
With his specific performance and its effects on other people, Falling Man is a symbol rather than an actual character; he mirrors some of the novel's important themes, such as the relationship between reality and its procession in the media (cf. 7.2) or the possibilities and limitations of art (cf. 7.3).

7. Themes and Motifs

7.1 "In the Ruins of the Future" – Terrorism, Plot and the Counternarrative

The topic of terrorism has played an important role in Don DeLillo's writing for many years. In his novel *Mao II* (1991) he had the main character, novelist Bill Gray, state the provocative opinion that there is a parallel between novelists and terrorists, and that terrorists have prevailed: " 'Years ago I used to think it was possible for a novelist to alter the inner life of the culture. Now bomb-makers and gunmen have taken that territory. They make raids on human consciousness.' " (Don DeLillo, *Mao II*, p. 41) Ten years later, two months after 9/11, DeLillo published a long essay about the events, "In the Ruins of the Future: Reflections on Terror and Loss in the Shadow of September"; it not only presents his thoughts on terrorism, its reasons and effects, but also a personal insight into the tragedy, as DeLillo's nephew and his family (who lived near the World Trade Center) were almost killed when the towers col-

lapsed. DeLillo also describes his impressions of Ground Zero, as he went to the site a few days after the attacks.
In the essay the author takes up fictional Bill Gray's train of thought in stating that: "Today, again, the world narrative belongs to terrorists." He describes the overpowering effects of terror:

> "Terror's response [to America's dominant role in the world] is a narrative that has been developing over years, only now becoming inescapable. It is our lives and minds that are occupied now. This catastrophic event changes the way we think and act, moment to moment, week to week, for unknown weeks and months to come, and steely years. Our world, parts of our world, have crumbled into theirs, which means we are living in a place of danger and rage."

In *Falling Man* we can see these theoretical reflections turned into fiction. There are numerous indications of public life in New York changing in the wake of the terror attacks, days and weeks after: The sight of police, state troopers and guardsmen in uniforms, "jungle camouflage in midtown Manhattan" (p. 42) becomes normality; many people leave the city, others (like Nina) suppress their fears and stay, like a kind of statement; still, they react with outrage when reminded of the events by Falling Man's performance (cf. pp. 40–41). Some people read poems, as Lianne tells Martin: " 'People I know, they read poetry to ease the shock and pain, give them a kind of space, something beautiful in language, [...] to bring comfort or composure.' " (pp. 52–53)
As for the individual characters in the novel, each of them is in one way or another affected by the events, even the small children, who keep searching the skies for the enemy in fear of more terror. Each life is being tested (cf. 6. Characters).
The essay "In the Ruins of the Future" also presents DeLillo's view on the terrorists ("Them") by describing the stark contrast between them and the Western world ("Us") that they fight against: "We are rich, privileged and strong, but they are willing to die. This is the edge they have, the fire of aggrieved belief." This argumentation anticipates Martin's statements in *Falling Man*. And the following description in the essay clearly foreshadows the character and development of Hammad in the novel:

> "The terrorist, planted in a Florida town, pushing his supermarket trolley, nodding to his neighbour, lives in a far narrower format. This is his edge, his strength. Plots reduce the world. He builds a plot around his anger and our indifference. He lives a certain kind of apartness, hard and tight."

It is the reducing of the world to a single line, the tunnelled vision, the "intensity of plot" (as DeLillo has called it in an interview) and, most important, the feeling of being wrapped up in a group of "brothers" we see in Hammad that DeLillo writes about five and a half years before the publication of *Falling Man*:

> "At a certain point he [the terrorist] and his brothers may begin to feel less motivated by politics and personal hatred than by brotherhood itself. They share the codes and protocols of their mission here and something deeper, a vision of judgment and devastation."

The people around him, the people he is going to kill – the terrorist does not see them anymore, "[...] there is no defenceless human at the end of his gaze." Later, in *Falling Man*, Amir will talk to Hammad like that, only more ruthlessly:

> "Amir said simply there are no others. The others exist only to the degree that they fill the role we have designed for them. This is their function as others. Those who will die have no claim to their lives outside the useful fact of their dying." (p. 224)

There is another important aspect in DeLillo's essay, referring to people's, and especially the writer's, reaction to terrorist acts: "The narrative ends in the rubble and it is left to us to create the counternarrative." This can be manifold: Stories we have learned, seen, heard about the day, objects that are shown, memorials, photos of missing persons, reproductions in the media such as the internet, even false or imagined memories – all these things are needed to be set against the incomprehensible terrorist plot, to make the "defenceless human" visible again. In *Falling Man*, Florence and Keith, for example, create the counternarrative, the one by the continuous relation of her escape from the tower, the other by listening intently, sharing the experience and at least partly allowing his own memories to enter his mind again. The Alzheimer patients create the counternarrative: "They wrote about the planes. They wrote about where they were when it happened. They wrote about people they knew who were in the towers, or nearby, and they wrote about God." (p. 76)
In this context, DeLillo's essay gives some programmatic sentences about the writer's role, indirectly showing the difference between literary and nonfictional treatment of the topic. The writer (of literature) does not give the sheer facts nor does he reveal the historic, political, religious background in detail. "The writer begins in the towers, trying to imagine the moment, desperate-

ly." He tries to respond to the singularity of the event not by presenting as many data and pieces of information as possible, but by re-establishing humanity, even beauty in it. "There is something empty in the sky. The writer tries to give memory, tenderness and meaning to all that howling space." In creating the stories of Keith, Lianne and the others, the author of *Falling Man* has done just that.

7.2 Media, Image and Reality

At the beginning of chapter 6 of the novel, the narration returns to the moment when Keith, covered in ash and blood, appears at Lianne's door after his escape from the burning tower. Although in shock herself, Lianne does what is necessary, she tries to call a doctor or a hospital and then: "She turned off the TV set, not sure why, protecting him from the news he'd just walked out of, that's why" (p. 109). This quotation comprises different layers of meaning, considering the question of the media – another theme important to DeLillo's writing in general and this novel in particular.

First it reminds the reader of the actual historic day of September 11, 2001: Beside being a terrible tragedy, the terror attacks on the World Trade Center and the Pentagon were also one of the biggest media spectacles of all time, a mass disaster immediately absorbed into a permanent time loop of media broadcast. Thus 'fictional' Lianne, just like many of the 'real' readers, could watch it as it happened.

Secondly, the quotation shows how difficult it is for Lianne to distinguish between the real situation and its presentation on TV. The simultaneity of reality and media image is complete; the image even seems to have taken the place of the original. This kind of perception also appears in another situation towards the end of the novel: Lianne watches a poker tournament on TV while Keith – at home on one of his visits from Las Vegas – is sitting in the next room sorting through his mail. "She hit the mute button and looked at the players seated around the tables as the camera slowly swept the room and she realized that she was waiting to see Keith." (p. 271) Lianne is ready to see the 'mediated' Keith rather than the 'flesh-and-blood' Keith next door, the representation has become the real. (This is opposed to Keith's way of watching poker on TV, described earlier in the book: "He watched without interest. It wasn't poker, it was television." [p. 146] He very well separates the game from its presentation.) Strangely enough, Lianne even seems to realize her somewhat twisted perception and turns it into a kind of self-ironic little fantasy – but remains absorbed in her screen-searching:

> "She imagined herself in cartoon format, a total fool, hurrying to Justin's room, hair flying, and dragging him out of bed and standing him up in front of the screen so he could see his father, *Look*, in Rio or London or Las Vegas. His father was twenty feet away at the desk in the next room reading bank statements and writing checks. She watched a little while longer, looking for him, and then she stopped." (p. 271)

In the context of this part of the novel, Lianne's attitude certainly also mirrors the growing alienation between her and Keith, who seems to be little more than a fleeting image for her and Justin.
The omnipresence and dominance of the television has always been one of DeLillo's concerns; with the subject of September 11 and its aftermath chosen for the novel *Falling Man*, it has of course become inevitable. When Keith and Lianne are talking, they are watching a TV programme without sound about some military preparations (probably preceding the war in Afghanistan); the two of them are hardly able to concentrate on their conversation, but do not turn the volume up either as if trying to shut the images (here, meaning reality of a war to come) out of their private lives (cf. pp. 165–166). When on her own, Lianne repeatedly watches the TV footage of the planes crashing into the towers; it is an ambiguous fascination: "Every time she saw a videotape of the planes she moved a finger toward the power button on the remote. Then she kept on watching." (p. 169) Here she seems to confirm the opinion of Murray, one of several characters in DeLillo's novel *White Noise* (1985), who discuss the question why people are so intrigued by catastrophes when they see them on TV:

> " 'Because we're suffering from brain fade. We need an occasional catastrophe to break up the incessant bombardment of information. [...] The flow is constant. [...] Words, pictures, numbers, facts, graphics, statistics, specks, waves, particles, motes. Only a catastrophe gets our attention. We want them, we need them, we depend on them.' " (Don DeLillo, *White Noise*, p. 66)

However, by showing Lianne almost physically absorbing the images of the catastrophe ("this was the footage that entered the body", p. 169), DeLillo goes one step further: This, for once, is not the medium replacing the real event, but the medium – in its original meaning – being the instrument (the 'means') to gradually understand, accept, even appreciate reality (e.g. Keith's survival). DeLillo picks up a train of thought stated in his essay "In the Ruins of the Future", where he explains that the events of September 11 were too powerful to be altered by their relentless media reproduction; it was impossible for the viewers at that time to resort to a detached perspective:

> "The event dominated the medium. It was bright and totalising and some of us said it was unreal. When we say a thing is unreal, we mean it is too real, a phenomenon so unaccountable and yet so bound to the power of objective fact that we can't tilt it to the slant of our perspective."

Thus Lianne's and Keith's jointly watching the TV footage mirrors their dawning knowledge of the real impact behind the smooth images, the acceptance of what has really happened:

> "He said, 'It still looks like an accident, the first one. Even from the distance, way outside the thing, how many days later, I'm standing here thinking it's an accident.'
> 'Because it has to be.'
> 'It has to be,' he said.
> 'The way the camera sort of shows surprise.'
> 'But only the first one.'
> 'Only the first,' she said.
> 'The second plane, by the time the second plane appears,' he said, 'we're all a little older and wiser.'" (pp. 170–171)

"Natura morta" (representative of Morandi's way of painting as described in the novel)

7.3 Mortality and Art

Death, dying or, more generally, mortality is another theme that pervades the novel; it is even inherent in its title, *Falling Man*. There are, of course, the thousands of victims of the terror attacks that are a looming presence in the narration, either in Keith's experiences (when he sees people jump from the towers and his friend Rumsey die) or in Lianne's preoccupation with the news stories about the victims or in Florence's walk to the church where she sees the memorials of the dead and photos of the missing. Certainly one of the most haunting pieces of the book is the description of Keith's impressions when he sees Ground Zero two or three days after the attacks:

> "The dead were everywhere, in the air, in the rubble, on rooftops nearby, in the breezes that carried from the river. They were settled in ash and drizzled on windows all along the streets, in his hair and on his clothes." (p. 30)

The theme also occurs in the individual lives of the characters. Lianne's father's suicide is a permanent echo from the past. There is no doubt about the dooming fate of the Alzheimer patients, some of them disappear from the group in the course of the sessions. Proud and confident Nina deplores time passing so quickly when she speaks about her renewed passport: " 'Ten years come and gone, like a sip of tea.' " (p. 143); she later dies, leaving another gap in Lianne's life. On a more metaphorical level, relationships between characters can be seen as moribund or dying: Lianne's and Keith's, Keith's and Justin's, Keith's and Florence's, even Nina's and Martin's.
The connection between mortality and art is directly evoked in the book. First of all, the works of the Italian painter Giorgio Morandi play an important role. Morandi (1890–1964) specialized in still lifes; in minimalist simplicity, almost reaching abstraction, he painted (among others) kitchen objects, the same familiar bottles, tins, vases again and again. In the novel, he is one of Lianne's, Nina's and Martin's favourite artists; Martin owns two of his paintings, which he has given to Nina to hang on a wall in her apartment. When during the three characters' long conversation Lianne and Martin have a closer look at one of the paintings, they see the twin towers in two of the taller objects depicted in it – thus, of course, showing first of all how much the impact of the terror attacks dominates people's perception. However, it is Nina who rejects a 'translation' of the painting's objects into a concrete, physical shape, but rather sees an underlying universal idea: " 'It's all about mortality, isn't it? [...] Being human, being mortal.' " (pp. 139–140). Human mortality is reflected in the immortality of art. After Nina's death Lianne goes

to an exhibition of Morandi's paintings in Chelsea, experiencing the very feeling Nina mentioned: Looking intently at the paintings evokes memories, brings Nina to life again. For Lianne, the paintings are no longer just pieces of art that she can sit back and read about in a catalogue: "Nothing detached in this work, nothing free of personal resonance." (p. 267) This paradoxical feeling – bringing to life by reminding of the dead – is heightened by the Italian title of all paintings, *Natura morta*: "Even this, the term for still life, yielded her mother's last days." (ibid.)

The character of David Janiak, Falling Man, is the most obvious representative of art in the novel, staging his performance unexpectedly in front of involuntary audiences all over New York. His artistic concept and intentions are never revealed in the text, it is left to Lianne, the media, finally the reader to speculate on them. In Falling Man's performance the aspects of mortality and art are strongly connected. He enacts a photo that, although being an image of an authentic, terrible event, the imminent death of a man, in itself reflects high artistic perfection, even beauty, and has since then become an icon. Lianne expresses this contradiction when she does an internet research on Falling Man and comes up with the photo: "Headlong, free fall, [...] and this picture burned a hole in her mind and heart, dear God, he was a falling angel and his beauty was horrific." (p. 282) With his perfomance Falling Man demonstrates the true power of art by regaining the subtext and making human life falling towards death visible again. Thus he undermines the efforts and effects of modern mass media, which either delete certain images or endlessly repeat them until they lose any reference to reality and are literally frozen to smooth symbols (cf. 7.2 and 7.4). It is no surprise, then, that Falling Man rejects every offer to be absorbed by mainstream culture, although he cannot avoid becoming a topic of abstract panel discussions himself: "Falling Man as Heartless Exhibitionist of Brave New Chronicler of the Age of Terror" (p. 280). He simply stops his performances; maybe he has realized the limitations of his idea of art – or the gradual loss of its immediate impact on the viewers.

At this point the more general question of DeLillo's artistic concept may arise, the way he he creates his "counternarrative" (cf. 7.1) in this novel. As a writer, he is concerned with language, with changing the seeing and (hopefully) understanding into the speaking and then sharing this experience with his readers. An adequate expression may be found in the description of the Alzheimer patients' writing group: "[...] there were a thousand high times the members experienced, given a chance to encounter the crossing points of insight and memory that the act of writing allows" (p. 78). Just like his fictional character Falling Man, DeLillo has refrained from repeating the well-known, ever-processed data, facts and names and tried instead to trace the enormous impact of the historical event in the ordinary lives of a few characters, to instil life (and death, come to that) into facts and numbers. Interestingly enough, DeLillo compares his writing of the novel, its specific structure of breaking up story lines and perspectives and putting them together again in different orders, with the work of a painter, thus closing the circle to Morandi:

> "I was writing out of sequence and then began to fit the parts together and, as I say, look for these balances and the way in which the past yields the present and vice versa. Sometimes this is what I think novelists do that makes them similar to painters. Abstract painters in particular. Looking for things in one part of a canvas that echo things in another part of the canvas." (Interview with Mark Binelli, 2007)

7.4 Memory and Loss

The theme of 'memory' is like a spider's web in the novel – each character is in some way or other entangled in it. Lianne's father, Jack Glenn, killed himself before his diagnosed dementia could take over; Lianne lives in constant fear of that disease and goes through regular tests, at the same time she accompanies a group of Alzheimer patients on their way into final amnesia. Nina struggles not only with her physical ailments but also with the first mental "erosions", the forgetting of names or locations of objects she has put away. Martin is fond of a snapshot of Nina and himself from the very beginning of their relationship, the only picture he keeps on his walls. For Florence, meeting Keith means having the chance to relive and memorize an experience that is almost too difficult to bear. Keith willingly goes along this journey into their "crossing memories" (p. 71), but tries to shut out completely the first part of that journey, memories of Rumsey's death in the tower. Justin stubbornly denies that part of the 'universal memory' his child's mind cannot cope with, the collapsing of the towers. Hammad eradicates whole parts of his memory, family, girlfriend, to become a single-minded, tunnel-visioned radical. And finally, Falling Man in his performance continuously reminds his audience of those horrible images that they would rather delete from public memory completely.

On the level of the individual, memory is equalled with the command of one's personal history and thus forms the basis for each character's identity; its loss means the disappearance of that character, literally and figuratively.

In the story, the reader witnesses attempts to fight against that loss. The Alzheimer writing group, for example, provides the patients with a possibility to slow down that process. For Lianne, who keeps all their writings neatly filed away, it is an equally important therapy, as in the group "the thing that killed her father" (p. 77) and thus her most haunting fear comes alive, easier to face, if not overcome.

The old passport photos from Martin's collection can be compared with the writings; they represent something beyond the bureaucratic need – an invitation for the viewer to see the lives and fates behind them. The invention of a context already saves those people from falling into oblivion.

The events of September 11 have certainly become part of the collective memory of a city, a society, maybe the world, forever – in countless images and illustrations. However, after the first waves of shock and dismay, the impact of reality underneath the surface of those images may have become lost to those people who were not directly affected by the terrorist acts and their effects. Within the fictional world of the novel, Falling Man's performances (as mentioned above) force his audience to regain not only lost or suppressed images, but also the knowledge of lives (and lives lost) behind them – and, come to that, DeLillo's whole novel, the act of writing, revitalizes parts of his readers' memory that they have perhaps detached themselves from (cf. 7.3 Mortality and Art).

7.5 Solace and Relief

The novel *Falling Man* shows the invasion of a dramatic event in the lives of a few individual characters and their different ways of coping with it, the focus being on the development of the main characters, Keith and Lianne. They go through different stages, their relationship changing from separation to closeness to distance again.

In the immediate aftermath of the catastrophe Keith and Lianne impulsively lay aside all the problems and differences that made it impossible for them to live together in the past. Both of them seem to seek solace in the physical presence of the other (with having sex only being a part of that). However, they do not pass beyond that stage of being physically together as a family (with their son). Probably because of their tormenting arguments in the past ("'It practically killed us'", p. 95), Keith in particular does not believe in finding relief in talking (for example about his experiences in the tower). Lianne accepts this attitude, even tries to persuade herself that they do not need abundant talking, which she automatically equals with conflict ("'The every-

day friction. The every-word every-breath schedule we were on before we split' ", ibid.). This arrangement, this readiness to sink into their little lives (cf. ibid.), is only half-hearted and not completely honest. Both Keith and Lianne find outlets for their inner pressure and turmoil – and both turn to the power of words after all, only in different ways and with different people.
When, on another impulse he cannot explain, Keith does not leave Florence after he has given back the briefcase, he takes the chance to open up. With Keith, this does not necessarily mean that he does the talking, but his intent listening to Florence's story, his need to find his own place in it, in a way unties a knot; after that he is even able to talk himself: "The talk continued, touching on marriage, friendship, the future. He was an amateur at this but spoke willingly enough. Mostly he listened." (p. 114) Sharing physical nearness, having sex and enjoying it, develops almost naturally, without arguing right or wrong, from Keith's and Florence's sharing their experiences. It is only when their affair leaves the stage of being relief and Florence starts to make plans for their future, even puts forward certain demands, that Keith decides to end it – allegedly because of his renewed role as husband and father, but basically because of his insecurity about any kind of commitment.
Lianne, always the one more willing and ready to talk, finds it difficult and fruitless to speak with her mother – mainly because of their strained relationship, Nina's dominance and fixed image of Keith. When her mother and Martin argue, Lianne listens but does not join in the conversation, except for some light banter. She rather keeps her emotions for the writing group of Alzheimer patients that she takes care of. It is very obvious that these meetings are as rewarding for Lianne as they are for the patients – although their terrible illness and ever-deteriorating state reminds Lianne of her father. When she encourages the patients, their writings are a kind of surrogate relief for her: "She wanted to hear everything, the things everybody said, ordinary things, and the naked statements of belief, and the depth of feeling, the passion that saturated the room." (p. 77) In a way, they talk and express for her what she feels and cannot utter – even the strong feelings towards the terrorists that she almost forces the group to write about: "Lianne suspected what this was. It was a response defined in terms of revenge and she welcomed this, the small intimate wish, however useless in a hellstorm." (p. 81) Later, when Lianne is asked by the group to tell them where she was when the attacks happened, she is finally able to open up herself, to pour out all the experiences, feelings, fears that have piled up:

> "The words came fast. She recalled things she didn't know she'd absorbed [...]. She wanted to stay focused, one thing following sensibly upon another. There were moments when she wasn't talking so much as fading into time, dropping back into some funneled stretch of recent past. They sat dead still, watching her." (p. 160)
> "Tell them everything, say everything." (p. 161)

It is almost like a therapeutic session, roles reversed, the patients being the psychologists.
Three years later, Keith and Lianne go more or less separate ways again. Although they have kept up their marriage, they are far from feeling the physical closeness they needed so badly after September 11; on the contrary, it seems as if Keith cannot wait to return to Las Vegas – the place he feels more familiar with than his so-called home with wife and son in New York: "When his plane came down over the desert he could easily believe that this was a place he'd always known." (p. 251) The family status seems fragile, reflecting the overall feeling, expressed by Lianne: " 'I know that most lives make no sense. I mean in this country, what makes sense?' " (p. 273) The events of 9/11 and their effects are still present in people's lives (anti-war demonstration, TV footage on US army, obituary of Falling Man, political discussions) but both Lianne and Keith are detached from the political side and concerned with reconstructing their personal lives from the ruins, so to say. They are both looking for spiritual guidance, or a kind of sanctuary, and the one's search for individual solace is very similar to the other's, in so far as in both cases it has little to do with other people, but with obsessions they have known for some time. However, their obsessions are very different, and the one has no understanding whatsoever of the other's.
Keith has finally returned to poker full-time. He finds everything he needs in that game and its surroundings: a fixed setting, anonymous contestants, rules that everyone has to follow, physical and mental discipline, control, total dependence on himself, his abilities and decisions:

> "Then, always, in the crucial instant ever repeated hand after hand, the choice of yes or no. Call or raise, call or fold, the little binary pulse located behind the eyes, the choice that reminds you who you are. It belonged to him, this yes or no [...]." (p. 269)

Here he has established an identity, found a mode of existence that is not as complicated and not as threatening as the everyday life he has long tried to lead but has never been sure of. For Keith, the unhealthy, strained, almost autistic life of the professional poker player is a relief and an apt armour

against other people's views, expectations, demands – and against fears and memories stemming from his worst moments in the tower.
Lianne follows a different but similarly self-centred track; she does not seem to have any close relations except to Justin. In her search of some rest for her troubled mind, she has started to go to church. (It is a church she knows from Rosellen, a member of the writing group, very dear to Lianne.) She still grapples with the question of God and religious belief – thinking she cannot share it – but she enjoys the church as a place, a building with a special kind of atmosphere and history. Instead of feeling the presence of God, she senses the reassuring spiritual presence of other people, especially of those who died:

> "She felt the dead, hers and unknown others. [...] She felt the dead in the walls, over decades and centuries. There was no dispiriting chill in this. It was a comfort, feeling their presence, the dead she'd loved and all the faceless others who'd filled a thousand churches. They brought intimacy and ease, the human ruins that lie in crypts and vaults or buried in churchyard and plots." (pp. 297–298)

All preoccupations are here again: thoughts of death, memories of the past, lives in ruins. However, Lianne seems to have slowly gained a different attitude towards them, she is able to accept the solace of the moment, the rituals of the liturgy among the other churchgoers, without the arguing of the abstract questions. She has finally reached a point where she at least sometimes can lay those 'demons' to rest, "in reliable calm", on her own.

Appendix

1. Structure in Overview

K = Keith
L = Lianne
H = Hammad

date and time given in the text: **bold print**
date and time estimated: in ( )

Part One: Bill Lawton

Ch.	Action	Time
1	**Keith** escapes from north tower after terror attack	Sept 11, 2001
2	**Lianne** thinks of the early times of her marriage; receives a postcard from a friend in Rome; speaks with her mother Nina about Keith, her marriage, the new situation	(8 years ago) **three days after the planes** (Monday after the attacks)
3	**Keith** in hospital, treated by a young doctor **Lianne** with Isabel, mother of the Siblings, talking about the children's strange behaviour **Lianne** watched by Keith in their bedroom **Keith** in hospital inside a scanner **Lianne** looks at the photo of a terrorist **Lianne** on the phone with her editor, Carol Shoup **Lianne** asks Keith why he has come to her flat **Keith** in hospital, having surgery on his wrist **Lianne** on the street, reflecting on her situation **Keith** goes to his old apartment to get some personal things, passes Ground Zero	(day of the attacks) (some days after the attacks) (day of the attacks) (some days after the attacks) (day of the attacks) (some days after…) (two or three days after the attacks)

4	**Lianne's** Alzheimer patients writing group introduced; they want to write about the planes **Keith** back in the family's apartment; he sorts through his mail **Lianne** goes to Grand Central Station to pick up her mother; she sees Falling Man for the first time **Lianne** reflects on her marital situation **Keith** examines the briefcase he has taken out of the tower **Lianne** talks with Isabel again, who mentions the kids talking about "Bill Lawton" **Keith** wakes up because of music in the house **Lianne** tries to talk with Justin (binoculars) **Keith** doing rehab exercises for his wrist injury ***flashback:*** **Lianne** thinks of her father, who committed suicide **Lianne** at her mother's flat, after Martin's arrival; argument about the terrorists	(some days after the attacks) (two or three days after the attacks) **ten days after the planes** (some days after the attacks) (the week after the attacks) (24 and 16 years ago) **Monday** after the attacks (cf. ch. 2)
5	**Keith** returns the briefcase to Florence Givens; they talk **Lianne** thinks about Keith in the past and now **Lianne** meets the doctor of the Alzheimer patients **Lianne** with her writing group; they speak and write about the planes **Keith** reflects on his present situation **Lianne** awake at night, angry about the loud music from a neighbour's flat **Lianne** and Keith in the kitchen, talking about Justin and the Siblings ("Bill Lawton")	(the week after the attacks) **fifteen days after the planes**
On M.str.	**Hammad** in Hamburg, with other Arab students	(about two years before the attacks)

Part Two: Ernst Hechinger

Ch.	Action	Time
6	**Lianne** takes care of Keith, who has come to her after his escape from the towers	September 11
	Keith is at Florence's flat again; they start an affair	(the week after the attacks)
	Lianne's writing group: deterioration of the patients' health	
	Lianne and Keith walking down the stairs; Keith kicks the door of the neighbour with the loud music	
	flashback: the poker nights at **Keith's** apartment	(the year before the attacks)
	Lianne, Keith and Justin at the table, discussing a trip and the children's stories about the planes	(a few weeks after the attacks)
	Keith sees a woman on horseback in the street	
	flashback: **Lianne** thinks of Keith's hostile behaviour shortly before their separation	**one and a half years ago**
	Lianne and Keith in a taxi, embracing; she thinks about their present situation	(in the weeks after the attacks)
	Keith is still doing his wrist exercises	
	Keith at Florence's flat; they speak about future plans	
7	**Lianne**, her mother, Martin at Nina's flat, continuing the political argument	(Monday after the attacks; cf. ch. 2,4)
	Lianne with Keith and Justin in the living-room, watching poker on TV	(some time after the attacks)
	Lianne confronts her neighbour Elena about the music, tries to hit her	
	flashback: **Keith** remembers his poker friend Rumsey and his idiosyncrasies	(before the attacks)
	Keith and Lianne speak about her action towards Elena and its reasons and effects *(dialogue)*	(some time after the attacks)
	Lianne's writing group: she tells the Alzheimer patients where she was when "it" happened	(some weeks after the attacks)
	Keith wonders about his development	(the year before the attacks)
	flashback: **Keith** thinks about the abilities of one of the poker players, Terry Cheng	

	flashback: **Lianne** thinks of herself as a child, of her father telling her about his first meeting with her mother **Lianne** tells Keith about her father's suicide **Keith** with Florence at Macy's to look for a mattress; Keith fights with a man **Lianne** keeps watching the TV footage of the terror attacks; watches with Keith once	**when she was twelve years old** (some weeks after the attacks)
8	**Keith** thinks about his affair with Florence after he has left her flat **Lianne** meets Carol Shoup, is angry as she has not got the offer to edit a book about terrorism **Lianne's** writing group: Rosellen S. had to leave **Keith** goes to a gym to start work-out **Lianne** at her mother's flat after Martin has left; they talk about Martin's past *flashback:* the poker group **Lianne** meets Elena in the basement; they do not talk to each other **Lianne** fetches Justin from the Siblings' flat; she intimidates Katie	(weeks after the attacks) (Monday after the attacks; cf. ch. 2,4,7) (the year before the attacks) (weeks after the attacks)
9	*parallel story lines:* **Lianne** walks home after a session of her writing-group, passes the church that Rosellen went to for help **Keith** walks with Justin after he has left Florence for good; they want to meet Lianne **Lianne** notices Falling Man on a platform **Keith** talks with Justin, thinks of telling Lianne about Florence **Lianne** watches Falling Man with other people around; he does not jump yet **Keith** and Justin still trying to meet Lianne; in the end they see her, run towards her **Lianne** sees Falling Man jump when a train comes; she flees the place; finally sees Keith and Justin run towards her	(see below) **thirty-six days after the planes**
In N.	**Hammad** in Florida, doing his flight-training, preparing for the attacks	(months, weeks before the attacks)

Part Three: David Janiak

Ch.	Action	Time
10	**Lianne** and Justin take part in an anti-war demonstration in New York **Lianne** has her brain tested and examined **Keith** is in Las Vegas, taking part in poker tournaments **Lianne** misses her mother, who died four months ago; she remembers seeing Martin at the memorial service; another political argument	three years after the attacks (four months before)
11	**Keith's** life at present; he has met Terry Cheng in Las Vegas **Lianne** asks Justin about her silver pen **Keith** talks with Terry Cheng during a break **Keith** calls Lianne after news about terrorists in a Russian school **Lianne** tells Keith about her medical tests **Keith** misses his son; he frequently phones Lianne	(about three years after the attacks)
12	**Lianne** goes to see a Morandi exhibition in Chelsea **Keith's** life as a professional poker player **Lianne** talks to Keith about their relationship and the family's future	
13	**Lianne** summoned for jury services, but not chosen for a trial against a woman associated with radical Muslims **Lianne** thinks of memories of her father and his suicide 19 years ago **Lianne** reads Falling Man's obituary in a paper, does a thorough computer research on him	(some weeks earlier) (three years after the attacks)
14	**Keith's** life in the casinos, his feelings, attitude towards the poker game **Lianne's** life in New York; she reflects on the question of religious belief, frequently goes to the church near the community centre, also continues her running **Keith** still doing his wrist exercises every day in his hotel room **Lianne** at church and at home, ready to go on living on her own, with her son	three years after the planes

In the H.C.	Hammad in the plane heading for the World Trade Center; it hits the north tower	minutes before the attack
	Keith's escape from the tower down the staircase after he has seen Rumsey die	immediately after the attack

2. Mark Binelli: "Intensity of a Plot. Interview with Don DeLillo" (2007) (extract)

[...]

Guernica: It would seem like writing about September 11th would be incredibly daunting. You've written about similar events in other novels, like the toxic cloud that passes over the city in *White Noise*, but there's generally a certain amount of irony and distance.

Don DeLillo: It is daunting, extremely. And the fact that I decided to go directly into the middle of the event didn't make it any easier. I didn't want to write a novel in which the attacks occur over the character's right shoulder and affect a few lives in a distant sort of way. I wanted to be in the towers and in the planes. I never thought of the attacks in terms of fiction at all, for at least three years. I was working on *Cosmopolis* on September 11th, and I just stopped dead for some time, and decided to work on the essay instead. Later, after I finished *Cosmopolis*, I had been thinking about another novel for some months when I began thinking about what would become *Falling Man*. What made it happen was a visual image: a man in a suit and tie, carrying a briefcase, walking through a storm of smoke and ash. I had nothing beyond that. And then a few days later, it occurred to me that the briefcase was not his. And that seemed to start a chain of thought that led to the actual setting of words on paper.

Guernica: Did this image just come out of nowhere, or from a photograph, or from stories of people you knew?

Don DeLillo: It just came out of nowhere, as these images tend to. It frequently happens that I begin a novel with just a visual image of something, a vague sense of people in three dimensional space.

[...]

Guernica: One of the characters in *Falling Man*, Hammad, is one of the 9/11 hijackers. Did you ever consider writing the entire book from his perspective? You've written so much about terrorism in the past.

Don DeLillo: I did not want to write a novel that had a great deal of political sweep. With the terrorist, I wanted to trace the evolution of one individual's passage from an uninvolved life to one that becomes deeply committed to a grave act of terror. And that's what I did. Not that I planned this beforehand. I mean, what I do, almost always, is I just start writing and through a character arrive at a sense of an overarching scheme, perhaps, under which he moves. With Hammad, I wanted to try to imagine how a man might begin as a secular individual and then discover religion, always through the power of deep companionship with other men. This is the force that drives him. Ultimately it's not religion, it's not politics and it's not history. It's a kind of blood bond with other men. And the intensity of a plot, which narrows the world enormously and makes it possible for men to operate without a sense of the innocent victims they plan to destroy.

Guernica: You often write about that sort of self-imposed asceticism. In *Falling Man*, there's a great scene in which some men involved in a weekly poker game begin to impose absurd limitations on what they can and cannot do, which ends up mirroring some of the rules imposed on the hijackers by their leaders.

Don DeLillo: That's true. Although I wrote the poker scene largely because I thought it was funny. I'm not sure I have a clear explanation for the asceticism of my characters in general. There are examples in a number of novels, including *Great Jones Street,* where a rock star abandons his career and lives in an obscure room somewhere in lower Manhattan. Maybe I have an ascetic gene that I haven't given full recognition to, except in my fiction.

Guernica: You don't personally yearn for those sorts of limits?

Don DeLillo: Only in a very general sense, in that I'm not very gregarious and don't mind spending periods of time alone.

Guernica: In a number of your past books, your characters have also expressed ambivalent feelings about the idea of terrorism. In the opening of *Players*, you describe the "glamour of revolutionary violence, the secret longing it evokes in the most docile soul..." And in *Mao II* one of the characters says of terrorists, "It's difficult when they kill and maim because you see them honestly now as the only possible heroes for our time... the way they live in the shadows, live willingly with death." Did what happened on September 11th change your own thoughts about terrorism?

Don DeLillo: No. I tend to write through character consciousness, and different people in my books have different feelings about this matter. One of the characters in *Falling Man*, Martin, makes a greater attempt to understand the complaints against the narcissistic heart of the West. The character he argues with, Nina, does not disagree with this in theory, but when the attacks occur, something else occurs, which is a terrible outrage.

Guernica: Did you struggle with similar responses yourself, after the attacks?

Don DeLillo: No, I didn't struggle. I knew I was totally opposed to what happened and to the reason for it.

[…]

Guernica: Going back to *Falling Man*, I was thinking about how Bin Laden's name is misheard as "Bill Lawton" by the kids, which makes him sound very mundane, and also how certain characters keep seeing the World Trade Center towers in a still life of bottles and other kitchen objects. Was this a conscious decision, taking an event that was so overwhelming to so many people and yoking it to the more mundane?

Don DeLillo: Absolutely. I was thinking about the impact of history on the smallest details of ordinary life, and I wanted to see if I could trace an individual's interior life, day-by-day and thought-by-thought. It occurs to me that this could be the novelist's initiative, even more than the story—to find the smallest intimate moments that people experience and share in conversation. I had none of this in mind. I just wanted to get the characters clear and, over time, create a balance, rhythm, repetition. This is what became satisfying to me. I was writing out of sequence and then began to fit the parts together and, as I say, look for these balances and the way in which the past yields the presence and vice versa. Sometimes this is what I think novelists do that makes them similar to painters. Abstract painters in particular. Looking for things in one part of a canvas that echo things in another part of a canvas.

[…]

From: Mark Binelli: "Intensity of a Plot. Interview with Don DeLillo", in: *Guernica Magazine*, July 2007,
www.guernicamag.com/interviews/373/intensity_of_a_plot

3. Selected Bibliography

Text Editions

DeLillo, Don, *Falling Man*, New York: Scribner, 2007.

– "In the Ruins of the Future: Reflections on Terror and Loss in the Shadow of September", in: *The Guardian*, December 22, 2001 (first published in *Harper's Magazine*, December 2001), www.guardian.co.uk/books/2001/dec/22/fiction.dondelillo (23.01.09).

– *Mao II*, London: Vintage, 1992.

– *White Noise*, New York: Penguin, 1986.

Secondary Sources

Amend, Christoph / Diez, Georg, „Ich kenne Amerika nicht mehr. Ein Gespräch mit Don DeLillo", in: *ZEITmagazin LEBEN*, Nr. 42, 11.10.2007, www.zeit.de/2007/42/Don-DeLillo-Interview (23.01.2009).

Begley, Adam, „DeLillo's 9/11 Resists Gravity", in: *The New York Observer*, May 8, 2007, www.observer.com/2007/delillo-s-9-11-resists-gravity?page=0%2C0 (23.01.2009).

Binelli, Mark, "Intensity of a Plot. An Interview with Don DeLillo", in: *Guernica Magazine*, July 2007, www.guernicamag.com/interviews/373/intensity_of_a_plot (23.01.2009).

Don DeLillo's America – A Don DeLillo Site, http://www.perival.com/0delillo/delillo/html. [Comprehensive website with bibliography, interviews, reviews, etc.]

Howe, Peter, "Richard Drew", in: *The Digital Journalist*, 2001, www.digitaljournalist.org/issue1001/drew.htm (23.01.2009).

Jones, Malcolm, "Up From the Ashes", in: *Newsweek Web Exclusive*, August 21, 2007, www.newsweek.com/id/34206/output/print (23.01.2009).

Junod, Tom, "The Falling Man", in: *Esquire* 140, September 2003, www.esquire.com/features/ESQ0903-SEP_FALLINGMAN (23.01.2009).

Leith, Sam, "After the Fall", in: *The Spectator*, May 19, 2007, www.spectator.co.uk/the-magazine/cartoons/30696/part_2/after-the-fall.thtml (23.01.2009).

Mars-Jones, Adam, "As His World Came Tumbling Down", in: *The Observer*, May 13, 2007, www.guardian.co.uk/books/2007/may/13/fiction.dondelillo (23.01.2009).

Raspe, Martin, "The Falling Man. Der 11. September in der Momentaufnahme", in: Irsliger, Ingo / Jürgensen, Christoph (eds.), *Nine Eleven. Ästhe-*

tische Verarbeitungen des 11. September 2001, Heidelberg: Winter, 2008, pp. 369–382.
Rich, Frank, "The Clear Blue Sky", in: *The New York Times*, May 27, 2007, www.nytimes.com/2007/05/27/books/review/Rich-t.html?pagewanted=1&_r=1 (23.01.2009).
TIME (special issue), September 11, 2001.

Model Questions and Answers

1. The novel *Falling Man* is about an important historic event. Describe the way DeLillo deals with 9/11 and explain the effects of his choice.

Don DeLillo has written about an event of global importance, but he does not give a detailed account of the facts or chronology of the terror attacks nor does he use the names of real people and places involved. There is only one mentioning of the term *World Trade Center* very late in the book, and one brief hint that the complete name of one of the terrorists is Mohamed Atta. Otherwise, all the familiar names and expressions are avoided, instead the characters speak about “the towers” and “the planes”.
The novel tells the rather intimate story of a few characters and the effects of that historic day on their lives and relationships. This way of dealing with the events is made even more forceful by the use of several perspectives, Keith’s, Lianne’s, Hammad’s, and indirectly Nina’s and Martin’s, which sometimes even contradict each other, thus presenting many facets of 9/11 and its context.
By focusing on the everyday lives of a restricted number of people and showing how the events influence these people’s present and future and also evoke memories and fears of their past, the author in a way ‘translates’ the abstract facts and well-known media images into the more palpable fates of ordinary individuals. The reader, who perhaps thinks he knows and has seen everything about 9/11, ideally gains a new and fresh perspective on the enormous impact of that national, maybe even global trauma.

2. Explain the specific structure of the novel’s narrative and its relevance for the story.

The story is not told in a traditional way and chronological temporal order; instead, the author splits up both the order and the perspective of the narrative. There is a continuous change between the perspectives of the two main characters, Keith and Lianne Neudecker. Additionally, a third story line presents the views and development of one of the terrorists, Hammad, his parts of the narrative closing each of the three parts of the book. As far as the time line is concerned, we have the date of September 11 as a starting point and follow Keith’s and Lianne’s development during the following three years, whereas Hammad’s story line takes us to that date from the other side, from roughly three years before. In the final chapter of the book, it has reached its

end – at the same time Keith's line returns to its beginning: The two characters, the two fates, terrorist's and victim's, are inseparably linked.
Within the individual story lines, especially Keith's and Lianne's, the chronology of events is disrupted again and again, with falling frequency as the story continues. The narration of the characters' present is fractured by flashbacks, memories of past events and situations turn up and their importance for the characters' lives and state of mind becomes obvious, sometimes (as in the case of Lianne's father's illness and suicide) almost overwhelming. When the lives of the main characters have seemingly become more settled in the last part of the book, the narrative looks more smoothly, its parts being longer, less fragmentary.
The specific narrative of the novel mirrors its main theme. It seems as if the tragic events on September 11 in a way have opened a lid, disclosing not only acute pains and scares of terrorism, but also cracking up the smooth surface of the characters' lives and letting all those disturbing memories, fears, experiences seep in that people have tried hard to bury. Literally nothing is safe and straight anymore, whole lives and relationships have to be rethought and restructured.

3. In which ways are Keith's, Lianne's and Justin's lives affected by the events of September 11?

As he was working in the north tower when the plane crashed into it, Keith is of course the one most directly affected by the terrorist act. He was right in the middle of death and destruction and – worst of all – he was not able to help his close friend Rumsey, who was fatally injured and died in his arms. Keith made it down the stairs and out of the towers with many other people, but the images keep following him ever since. Keith's life takes a completely new turn: He goes back to his wife and son without thinking about it, finding the quiet seclusion he obviously needs. Yet it is a more or less physical reunion, providing him with a sense of stability in everyday rituals and routine. Unlike the healing of his wrist injury, his mental convalescence remains incomplete. For a short time he has a relationship with Florence, another survivor, their only valid bond being their shared experiences in the burning tower. After a half-hearted attempt to find a new job, Keith finally drops out completely of his professional career, cuts off his relationship with Florence and again loosens his ties with his wife and son to enter his final retreat, the world of professional poker. Thus the events of September 11 and its aftermath have pushed Keith over the edge of that so-called normal life with a regular job and fulfilling the role of husband and father 'full-time'.
Lianne, too, gets very close to the actual events of September 11 when Keith turns up at her apartment, covered in ash and blood, materializing the im-

ages she has been watching with horror on TV. For her, that day marks the beginning of a period of time when her latent insecurity and unbalance are set free. Providing Keith with the peace and rest he needs, finding a new way of living with him, dealing with her son's strange behaviour and at the same time coping with her mother's illness and temper is sometimes more than she can handle. That is why she aggressively turns against her neighbour, by whose loud Arabic music she feels provoked. Terror, death and destruction that have hit her beloved city of New York revive her own private fears – of memory loss, relationships falling to pieces and, generally, mortality. Paradoxically, it is the writing group, the people who most personify those fears, that give Lianne the possibility to deal with the events of September 11 and their effects on her personal situation. Only gradually is she able to return to the relative, if delicate, calm of her pre-9/11 life with her son.
With the example of seven-year-old Justin (and his friends, the Siblings), the far-ranging impact of the terror attacks becomes very obvious: Suddenly the safety, stability and predictability of their children's lives are at stake. Although both Lianne and Keith carefully try to find a balance between telling their son what he is going to learn from people and media around him anyway and keeping him away from the worst images of the events, Justin stubbornly refuses to accept the reality of the disaster. Instead, he and his friends make every effort to regain control by scanning the skies with their binoculars for more planes and inventing their private "myth" of the terrorists, at the same time forming a strong circle of three, using their own secret code and trying to exclude the adults, who obviously are not trustworthy anymore. As for his individual situation (and as a specific result of the events of September 11), Justin has to get used to the continuous presence of his father again – and to the palpable fears of his mother (who, for example, refuses to take the underground).

4. Keith and Lianne choose different ways to find consolation and relief after the traumatic experiences of September 11. In that context, what does Keith's relationship with Florence mean to him? What is the importance of the Alzheimer writing group for Lianne?

When Keith returns the suitcase he has taken on his escape from the burning tower to its owner, Florence Givens, he finds out that she, too, was on the staircase among the hundreds of people who made it out of the tower. After some akward moments and small-talk with tea and cookies – a situation Keith normally avoids – the conversation turns to the situation in the tower and Florence gives a long, detailed, very emotional account of her way down the staircase. Although she does the talking, Keith takes part in the story – his body language and way of listening, his readiness to provide words she is

looking for and to remember his own position on the stairs making clear that this is his story, too. He seems to realize that, just like Florence, he must take the chance to go through the terrible event and face his own part in it. This sharing of their life-threatening experiences is the starting-point of an affair and it remains its strongest, if only foundation; they do have sex, but – at least in Keith's eyes – the most important aspect of those secret meetings is their common bond of "what they knew together, in the timeless drift of the long spiral down" (p. 172). For a short time, Keith finds in Florence what he does not find (and does not look for) in Lianne: not only physical closeness, but the possibility to speak about the horrible event and its meaning for his post-9/11 life. It is only when he feels that Florence wants to go beyond that sharing of experiences and makes plans for a future arrangement to continue their love affair that Keith (still believing he is going to fulfill the expectations of being a committed husband and father again) ends the affair.
Lianne's life has always been influenced by thoughts and fears of memory loss and threatening dementia, connected with mortality and death (e.g. her father's suicide). When starting the Alzheimer writing group, she has already chosen to go through her own kind of therapy – and, for that, is warned by Dr. Apter not to forget that it is for the patients first and not for her. Still, by giving in to the patients' wish to write and speak about "the planes", and even encouraging them to write something about the terrorists, too, Lianne experiences a kind of satisfaction that goes beyond her general fascination of seeing "something precious [...] the living breath of the thing that killed her father" (p. 77). When she listens to them, she can find in their writings and talking feelings, fears, passions that were triggered by the terror attacks and that she herself has not been able yet to speak about. In one of the later sessions the patients ask Lianne to write down and tell them where she was when the attacks happened; this is the culminating point of the story-line sessions, as she not only fulfills her part of the bond ("She owed them a story, didn't she?", p. 159), but in a way takes the role of a patient for some time, relieving her feelings, fears, emotional stress. The Alzheimer patients are the only people that Lianne can ever open up to completely.

5. Describe and discuss Keith's and Lianne's development in the last part of the novel. Consider their individual lives as well as their relationship.

The third and last part of the novel starts almost three years after the terror attacks on September 11. Despite his seeming resolve to lead an ordinary life as husband and father, Keith has entered a different path, becoming a full-time professional poker player. He spends most of his time in Las Vegas or other cities with big casinos and goes to New York occasionally for a few days

to see Lianne and Justin, holding contact mainly through frequent telephone calls. Keith's life in Las Vegas is characterized by a firm and simple structure, "standard methods and routines" (p. 251), dominated by the fixed times of the tournaments and almost completely locked up in rooms (poker rooms in casinos, hotel lobbies and rooms). In order to have as much time at the poker table as possible, Keith has distilled his needs down to the very essentials, having only two meals a day, drinking hardly any alcohol, needing only five hours' sleep. This parallels his cutting down his family life to the basic necessities of time and emotional commitment. He assures his wife of their economic security and promises he is not going to take any risk when playing poker, but although he misses his son and enjoys being on the phone with Lianne, he never stays with them in New York for more than three or four days and withdraws from any conversation that might take them to a deeper level of understanding and explanation of their existence or the future of their relationship respectively. For Keith, the poker game is the only way of living that provides him with the feeling of exercising control rather than being controlled by the force of events and people's expectations, as in the wake of September 11.
Corresponding with her husband's near-withdrawal from the family, Lianne's role and responsibility towards her son have grown again, she is "filling in [...] doing double duty", as she puts it herself (p. 238). With her mother dead and the Alzheimer group gone from her life, too, she is devoid of close relationships except with Justin. All her attempts to really understand and therefore accept Keith's obsession with poker are fruitless, especially as he does nothing to help her. The events of September 11 and the fears they have unfolded are still haunting her; she avoids taking the subway and when she accidentally finds a notice about Falling Man in a newspaper she cannot help doing a thorough research on his life and thus allowing her disturbing memories to rush in again. Additionally, she has developed a kind of obsession herself: She frequently goes to church and struggles with her longtime thoughts and doubts about God. Whereas being among the other churchgoers, following the rituals and enjoying the atmosphere give her a sense of calm and relief, she is too much of a sceptic to believe in God – all the time wishing she could find that spiritual strength, stability and self-righteousness that she sees in the sentence of the Koran, *This Book is not to be doubted*. Another attempt at gaining both physical and spiritual strength is Lianne's running, she even thinks of training for the marathon, "long-distance running as spiritual effort" (p. 297). In the end, she seems to see herself in a state of acceptance – of herself, her personal history, her wishes and unfulfilled dreams, her pseudo-marriage and her only existing relationship with her son; the question if that pre-9/11 state can (and should be) reached again is left open.

6. One of the story lines introduces Lianne's mother Nina and her lover Martin. What is their role in the story?

The role of the older of the two couples in the novel can be seen on two levels, politically and privately – and as proof of the difficulty to separate the two in the aftermath of 9/11.
A few days after the terror attacks, Nina and Martin (who has just returned from Europe) engage in a fervent argument about the terrorists and their motives. In this argument they take two totally opposed positions, which one could call (in a simplified way) the Western, pro-American and the anti-American stance. Nina condemns the terrorists' actions as cruel, irrational deeds that shall only divert people's attention from the shortcomings of the Third World countries. For her, they have no right to misuse the name of God in justifying killing and destruction. In contrast, Martin even states some kind of sympathy with the terrorists and their hatred of Western wealth, privileges and arrogance. For him, the Islamic (Eastern) countries have the right to reject Western influences and dominance and live according to their own standards and beliefs. He shows understanding of the terrorists' radical behaviour, his attitude, of course, being a strong provocation for his lover Nina. Thus, the author has used this couple to represent two opposing views of a global political discussion that has dominated the world for some time (symbolized, for example, by the term "clash of cultures").
On a more private level, Nina's and Martin's relationship can inevitably be compared with Keith's and Lianne's. Whereas the younger couple is brought together again for a short time after September 11, Nina's and Martin's estrangement mainly stems from their different attitudes described above. Yet despite their drifting apart on the outside (Nina even sends back the Morandi paintings Martin gave her), their inner bond never ceases to exist. This is made clear by Martin at the memorial service after Nina's death when he tells Lianne that he and Nina did not stop their talk, even if they did not speak anymore in the end: " 'Even when we no longer found agreeable things to say or anything at all to say. The conversation never ended.' " (p. 248) Their feelings for each other, the memories, the shared experiences, their special likings for art – this strong basis could not be destroyed by their political disagreement. This kind of relationship is contrasted to Keith's and Lianne's, who – despite their short intense reunion – again loosen their ties in the course of time, mainly because of their incapability of talking, sharing the same interests, opening up towards each other, understanding the other's preoccupations.

7. Each of the three parts of the novel has an appendix featuring Hammad, one of the terrorists, as the protagonist. What effect do these passages have on the novel as a whole? Do you see any importance in the author's decision to include the terrorist's perspective?

First of all, the passages with Hammad are an important part of the novel's structural principle: They add to the disintegration of the story's linearity and to the multi-perspectivity of the book. In addition to Keith's and Lianne's, Hammad's parts establish both a third story line and a third perspective. They also complement the temporal structure of the novel, as they refer to different points of time before the terror attacks on September 11, whereas Keith's and Lianne's stories are mainly followed after that day. When the last chapter of the book presents the overlapping of Hammad's and Keith's story and perspective in the detailed description of the actual plane crash and its immediate effects in the tower, the reader witnesses the culminating point of the novel – not only a temporal countdown from both sides of the event, but also a collision of live stories and terrorist's and victim's feelings and perspectives.

As for the content of the novel, DeLillo has chosen not to deal with the historic event in a broad, distant way but to concentrate on the outer and especially the inner development of a few characters affected by the events. With the description of the different stages in Hammad's last years, the author does not draw a particularly original portrait of the character, as the readers are well aware of that kind of 'conventional' behaviour of terrorists by now (the anonymous apartments, the inconspicuous life style and merging into their surroundings). However, by adding Hammad's perspective, i.e. telling his thoughts and feelings in an unfiltered way, the author has made a daring decision to have the readers enter the mental world and obsessions of a terrorist that most of them may find hard to imagine and reprehensible, perhaps even refuse to do so. DeLillo has often emphasized his interest in terrorism and the terrorist's mind; with Hammad, he has tried to follow the steps of an individual who at the beginning leads a secular life, with ambitions to have a job and a family, to the final stage of becoming a part of a small but strong, fanatic group whose atrocious act changes the lives of so many people for ever. Questionable as it may be, by making the reader know Hammad's feelings, convictions, also his doubts, and by bringing the reader to entering the terrorist's imagination in the last moments of his life, the author has given the abstract concept, maybe stereotype of a terrorist a human – but not humane – face.

8. The artist known as Falling Man is one of the most unusual characters in the novel. What part does he play within the story? How do you consider his performances?

Falling Man is not a mature character in the traditional meaning or reader's expectation but a kind of ghost-like figure that literally hovers in people's sight for a few moments only. Some information about his person is researched in the last part of the novel, after his death, by Lianne, who has seen him doing his performance twice in the course of the story. And it is this performance and not the person that is of importance, as it comprises several of the novel's themes. When Falling Man unexpectedly jumps from any kind of high structure, headfirst, held only by an invisible safety harness, he revives a sad and moving incident that has been turned into an abstract, even artistic image and as such has been banned from the media and public consciousness. He reclaims a place for those who died in the world of those who have survived and undermines the media's power over people's minds and memory, ignoring feelings of outrage and disgust in his audience. Lianne, when she witnesses one of Falling Man's performances for the second time, is spellbound, her reaction showing exactly this kind of image becoming reality again, in her case a very close and personal one: "But why was she standing here watching? Because she saw her husband somewhere near. She saw his friend, the one she'd met, or the other, maybe, or made him up and saw him, in a high window with smoke flowing out." (p. 212)

As for a full understanding of Falling Man and his intentions, the reader has to give in to speculations, just like Lianne, who finds the man elusive. As he is an artist, one can presume that his performances are part of a specific artistic concept. Besides re-creating reality and memories of a tragic event behind its processing in the media, he obviously puts great importance on the singularity of his 'work of art'. He wants it to remain not only a continuous reminder, but also an unexpected provocation and refuses to be drawn into the world and networks of mainstream culture. Yet he cannot prevent representatives of that culture from adopting him and his work and making it a subject for a panel discussion, neatly placing that disturbing phenomenon in prefabricated categories: "Falling Man as Heartless Exhibitionist or Brave New Chronicler of the Age of Terror". However, Falling Man evades any such kind of quick and definite interpretation, figuratively and literally, as in the end he stops his performances altogether.

9. Explain the significance of the Morandi paintings in the novel.

Paintings by the Italian artist Giorgio Morandi are mentioned and described a few times in the novel; they have a symbolic function on several levels. Two of Morandi's still lifes are hanging on one of the walls in Nina's apartment; they are a gift from her lover Martin. Towards the end of her life, in the process of their estrangement after their political argument, Nina makes Lianne send the paintings back to Martin; thus they symbolize the growing distance between the two lovers.

Nina, as a former professor of art, is an expert on Morandi's work. Lianne, too, likes the paintings in her mother's flat, and although they only show ordinary, everyday objects such as bottles, jugs, biscuit tins, she sees some mysterious, underlying meaning beyond the paintings' surfaces and is fascinated by them. This evocation of some human quality is emphasized by the name of the paintings, *Natura morta*. Lianne keeps those feelings, that changing flow of different impressions, to herself, she does not want to be 'lectured' by her mother, to have the paintings explained theoretically: "Let the latent meanings turn and bend in the wind, free from authoritative comment." (p. 15) Martin seems to be open to similar feelings: When, a few days after the terror attacks, he and Lianne are standing in front of the paintings, they can see the twin towers in two of the larger kitchen objects portrayed in one of the still lifes. This of course does not only show Martin's and Lianne's similarly emotional approach to the paintings, but also the strong impact of the tragic event on people's perception and sensation.

Nina rejects that kind of projection, but when she maintains that the paintings are a deeper and timeless image of human life and mortality in particular, it is not a contradiction, but rather a widening of the symbolic quality. This becomes particularly obvious when, after Nina's death, Lianne goes to see a Morandi exhibition in a gallery in Chelsea. On her close inspection, the paintings (some of which are variations of the ones in her mother's flat) yield lively memories of Nina and Martin, scenes Lianne has witnessed when her mother was still alive. In the paintings, those memories are immortalized forever. For Lianne, they have long lost their quality of works of art and become a kind of symbolic cover, a constant reminder of her mother and her important influence on her (Lianne's) life: "She was passing beyond pleasure into some kind of assimilation. She was trying to absorb what she saw, take it home, wrap it around her, sleep in it. There was so much to see. Turn it into living tissue, who you are." (p. 267)

10. Some critics have seen striking parallels in the developments of Keith and Hammad. Discuss similarities and differences between these two characters.

The two characters are explicitly and rather shockingly linked in the last chapter of the novel ("In the Hudson Corridor") that starts telling the flight of one of the planes towards the north tower, in Hammad's perspective, then suddenly switches to Keith's perspective within one long sentence about the impact of the plane crashing into the tower. Here the point of closest proximity, physically, between terrorist and victim is reached; Hammad's death marks the beginning of Keith's 'new' life.

Although their life lines are not synchronized in time, as Hammad's story leads up to and Keith's story starts from September 11, their developments and ways of life show some remarkable similarities. When we get to know them, they are (at least superficially) embedded in social structures and relations: Hammad has a girlfriend and lives with other students, Keith has returned to his wife and son after the shock of the terror attacks, even starts a relationship with another woman, Florence. Then both of them start on a kind of quest that makes them cut off or loosen the ties to their former existence, concentrating completely on their new ways of life, training for the terrorist act and the perfection of professional poker-playing respectively. In order to accomplish their different tasks, both characters succumb to strong rituals: Hammad in his hard physical training (e.g. in Afghanistan), Keith in the strict rules of his poker-playing or the physical exercises in a gym and repetitions of his wrist exercises. The two men ascetically reduce their lives: Hammad "prays and sleeps, prays and eats" (p. 176), Keith allows himself only five hours' sleep, has only two meals a day, hardly any alcohol. When he thinks of the poker game, he might just as well be the terrorist speaking: "Nothing else pertained. Only this had binding force. He folded six more hands, then went all-in. Make them bleed. Make them spill their precious losers' blood." (p. 293)

There is, however, a difference in what their lives are leading up to. Hammad, in his strong brotherhood with his fellow terrorists, is on a one-way road, so to say, his linear development running towards a defined ending that he knows and welcomes: "They felt the magnetic effect of plot. Plot drew them together more tightly than ever. Plot closed the world to the slenderest line of sight, where everything converges to a point." (pp. 221–222) For the terrorist, there is not a shadow of a doubt at the end, no questioning of the consequences of his deed, complete self-assurance, almost joyous expectancy of death as the door to "paradise". Keith's quest (and Lianne's, for that matter) does not follow any kind of plot in a straight and linear sense, he seems to move in the same circle of experiences and memories that he has entered after his escape from the tower – only he may find it easier to ignore it. Perhaps this is one of the reasons (referring to the narrative structure) why the last chapter of the book returns to the beginning: to mirror the circle that the victim – unlike the terrorist – has not been able to free himself from.

11. The events of September 11 have already been dealt with in many works of art, such as novels and films. Why do you think writers and artists in general go about that task to "present the unpresentable" (as one critic called it)?

No other event in recent history has been so thoroughly researched and medially reproduced as the terror attacks of September 11; the news, images, names of that day have become an important part of people's collective memory. It has been described and labelled in many different and general ways as the end of an era of Western dominance, beginning of the age of terrorism, culminating clash of cultures and so on. In our globalized world our understanding of the event has been formed and directed mainly by the data processed and multiplied in the media. At the same time very few people have been left emotionally cold and detached by the impact of the event; certainly many lives – even those who were not directly affected by the terror attacks and their consequences – have never been the same since then.

For every artist, it must be an immense challenge to find a language (in writing, filming, composing, painting) that convincingly and movingly expresses so many and completely different feelings such as sadness, anger, disorientation, patriotism, revenge (to name only very few). It seems as if, in their works, artists try to create structure where literally and figuratively so many things (artistic concepts, too) have been made into rubble. They also create the "counternarrative" (as DeLillo calls it) and claim their place to balance the extremist position of terrorism. At the same time their works – at the best of times – roughen the all-too-smooth images of that day and its aftermath spread by the media or bring to life those that have been omitted or forgotten.

Of course there has been the inevitable development (or danger?) that 9/11 is becoming a new kind of cultural myth, either stripped of its political and historic context or, in contrast, narrowed to single-minded political propaganda. When September 11 novels, for example, will have their own shelves in bookstores, 9/11 art (if we may call it that way) will have gone the same way as Falling Man in DeLillo's novel, who has finally become only a subject of a panel discussion.

12. Has reading *Falling Man* fulfilled or disappointed your expectations of a book dealing with September 11? Have you gained any new or different perspective on the event?

(Depending on the individual student's reception, many different answers are possible, for example:)

- Many details and images of the actual terror attacks, as presented at the beginning of the novel, are already too familiar.
- The last chapter gives a breathtaking, linguistically convincing description of how the situation in the towers may have been after the crash.
- The author's decision to focus on the fate of a few characters helps to understand the gravity of September 11, which might have become an abstract historic date for many of us.
- It is made difficult to identify or feel sympathy with the characters, who remain strangely detached from the reader.
- The portrayal of the terrorist Hammad is stereotyped and unoriginal; to give him such a big part in the story is a dangerous playing down of the terrorists' inhumanity.
- DeLillo's way of deconstructing the story lines and his unemotional, detailed style are uncomfortable and disquietening.
- With the description of the Alzheimer group the author has found a powerful image of the general dissolution of a world in the aftermath of 9/11.
- The novel does not create a context: There is no presentation of the serious political developments following the events of September 11 within the USA (e.g. highly criticized measures for home security) and worldwide (wars in Afghanistan, Iraq).

Acknowledgements

Bildquellennachweis

Cover: Interfoto Pressebild-Agentur, München
Seite 11: The Associated Press GmbH (Richard Drew), Frankfurt am Main
Seite 90: AKG, Berlin

Textquellennachweis

Seite 102: Mark Binelli: „Intensity of a Plot. Interview with Don DeLillo", in: *Guernica Magazine,* Juli 2007

Nicht in allen Fällen war es uns möglich, den Rechteinhaber ausfindig zu machen. Berechtigte Ansprüche werden selbstverständlich im Rahmen der üblichen Vereinbarungen abgegolten.